OF

MW01063418

NOTES

ncluding
- *Life and Background of the Author*
- *Introduction to the Novel*
- *Brief Summary of the Novel*
- *Chapter Summaries and Commentaries*
- *Literary Analysis*
- *Character Summations*

by
David C. Gild, Ph.D.
Yale University

Hungry Minds™

Best-Selling Books • Digital Downloads • e-Books • Answer Networks • e-Newsletters • Branded Web Sites • e-Learning

New York, NY • Cleveland, OH • Indianapolis, IN

CliffsNotes™ *The Mayor of Casterbridge*
Published by:
Hungry Minds, Inc.
909 Third Avenue
New York, NY 10022
www.hungryminds.com
www.cliffsnotes.com (CliffsNotes Web site)

ISBN: 0-8220-0816-5

Printed in the United States of America

10 9 8 7 6 5 4

1O/QS/RQ/QR/IN

Distributed in the United States by Hungry Minds, Inc.

Distributed by CDG Books Canada Inc. for Canada; by Transworld Publishers Limited in the United Kingdom; by IDG Norge Books for Norway; by IDG Sweden Books for Sweden; by IDG Books Australia Publishing Corporation Pty. Ltd. for Australia and New Zealand; by TransQuest Publishers Pte Ltd. for Singapore, Malaysia, Thailand, Indonesia, and Hong Kong; by Gotop Information Inc. for Taiwan; by ICG Muse, Inc. for Japan; by Norma Comunicaciones S.A. for Columbia; by Intersoft for South Africa; by Eyrolles for France; by International Thomson Publishing for Germany, Austria and Switzerland; by Distribuidora Cuspide for Argentina; by LR International for Brazil; by Galileo Libros for Chile; by Ediciones ZETA S.C.R. Ltda. for Peru; by WS Computer Publishing Corporation, Inc., for the Philippines; by Contemporanea de Ediciones for Venezuela; by Express Computer Distributors for the Caribbean and West Indies; by Micronesia Media Distributor, Inc. for Micronesia; by Grupo Editorial Norma S.A. for Guatemala; by Chips Computadoras S.A. de C.V. for Mexico; by Editorial Norma de Panama S.A. for Panama; by American Bookshops for Finland. Authorized Sales Agent: Anthony Rudkin Associates for the Middle East and North Africa.

For general information on Hungry Minds' products and services please contact our Customer Care department; within the U.S. at 800-762-2974, outside the U.S. at 317-572-3993 or fax 317-572-4002.

For sales inquiries and resellers information, including discounts, premium and bulk quantity sales and foreign language translations please contact our Customer Care department at 800-434-3422, fax 317-572-4002 or write to Hungry Minds, Inc., Attn: Customer Care department, 10475 Crosspoint Boulevard, Indianapolis, IN 46256.

For information on licensing foreign or domestic rights, please contact our Sub-Rights Customer Care department at 212-884-5000.

For information on using Hungry Minds' products and services in the classroom or for ordering examination copies, please contact our Educational Sales department at 800-434-2086 or fax 317-572-4005.

Please contact our Public Relations department at 212-884-5163 for press review copies or 212-884-5000 for author interviews and other publicity information or fax 212-884-5400.

For authorization to photocopy items for corporate, personal, or educational use, please contact Copyright Clearance Center, 222 Rosewood Drive, Danvers, MA 01923, or fax 978-750-4470.

Hungry Minds™ is a trademark of Hungry Minds, Inc.

CONTENTS

Introduction

    Early Education and Architectural Apprenticeship   5

    The Years as a Novelist (1867-1895)   6

    The Years as a Poet (1895-1928)   6

    The Mayor of Casterbridge and Hardy's Background   7

A Brief Synopsis   8

Summaries and Critical Commentaries   10

Critical Essays

    Structure   76

    Point of View and Style   78

    Theme   82

Character Analyses   84

INTRODUCTION

Thomas Hardy was born June 2, 1840, in the village of Upper Bockhampton, about three miles from the town of Dorchester in Southwestern England. The impressions of his early youth—the people, the events, the surrounding countryside—became part of the subject matter of his "Wessex" novels and stories. The town of Casterbridge itself, for example, is modeled after Dorchester.

Hardy's father was a builder and stone mason and was by no means wealthy. His mother loved reading, and under her care young Thomas was given an ample introduction to the classics, folk songs, ballads, and local stories and legends. Music was also a common feature of the Hardy household. Thomas's father taught him to play the violin, for he himself was violinist in the church choir and often played at parties, weddings, and festivals. Music was a great love throughout Thomas Hardy's life and often figures in his writing. At least three important scenes in *The Mayor of Casterbridge* involve music.

Early Education and Architectural Apprenticeship

Hardy did not study at a university. His formal education consisted of a year in a village school at Lower Bockhampton and additional private schooling in Dorchester during which he learned French and German. When he was sixteen, his father apprenticed him to a Dorchester architect, John Hicks, where he was taught architectural drawing for the restoration of churches and old houses. Indeed, this association taught him much of local family histories and folklore. When the day's work was completed, Thomas usually undertook advanced Latin studies and the task of teaching himself Greek.

In 1862 Hardy went to London as a draftsman and worked in the office of A. W. Blomfield, an architect. During this time he won a number of prizes for essays, and he began to steep himself in architectural and art studies, classic literature, contemporary poetry, and fiction. In 1867 he returned to Dorchester to a better position as a church-restorer with his former master, and began to write more steadily.

The Years as a Novelist (1867–1895)

From this time on, Hardy wrote poetry and novels, though he dedicated himself chiefly to the novel form until 1895. At first Hardy published anonymously, but as interest grew in his work, he began to write under his own name. His novels were published for the most part in serial form in well-known magazines both in England and America. His major novels are: *Under the Greenwood Tree* (1872), *Far from the Madding Crowd* (1874), *The Return of the Native* (1878), *The Mayor of Casterbridge* (1886), *The Woodlanders* (1887), *Tess of the D'Urbervilles* (1891), and *Jude the Obscure* (1895). His works were highly acclaimed (the success of *Far from the Madding Crowd* enabled him to give up architecture and to marry), but he also encountered literary hostility. *Jude the Obscure* received such harsh criticism that Hardy gave up the writing of novels entirely.

The Years as a Poet (1895–1928)

Hardy retired to his house in Dorchester and there turned to poetry almost exclusively. Before his death he completed over 800 poems and a long epic drama, *The Dynasts* (1908). His first marriage was not a happy one, but in 1914, two years after the death of his first wife, he married a second time. The remaining supremely happy years of his life were spent in matrimonial devotion and reticent tranquility.

The last two decades of Hardy's life were increasingly full of honors. With Meredith's death in 1909, he became undisputed holder of the title of greatest living man of letters, and in 1910 he was awarded the Order of Merit. His house, Max Gate, became a literary shrine, and there he received many visitors from all over the English-speaking world. He continued to

publish poetry well into the nineteen-twenties, even though he
was then over eighty. He died at the age of 87 on January 11,
1928.

The Mayor of Casterbridge and Hardy's Background

On every page of Hardy's Wessex novels is displayed
the influence of Hardy's upbringing, regional background, and
architectural studies. His characters are often primitive—as is
the case in *The Mayor of Casterbridge*—and exhibit all the
passions, hates, loves, and jealousies that rustic life seems to
inspire. Yet these characters are at all times real, for they are
based on people he had grown up with, people he had heard
about in legends and ballads, people whose tragic histories he
had unearthed during his early architectural apprenticeship.
There are also long, well-wrought, descriptive passages of the
surrounding countryside, the buildings, the roads, the commerce,
and the amusements that make up the environment of Casterbridge. It is Hardy's naturalness in handling this particular
environment, which he called "Wessex," that puts us at our ease
and infuses the work with a life and a reality all its own.

Hardy's philosophy dramatizes the human condition as a
struggle between man and man, and between man and his fate.
Usually it is fate—or the arbitrary forces of the universe—that
wins. Fate is all-powerful, and in its blindness human suffering
is of no importance. This malevolence of fate certainly seems at
times to be demonstrated in *The Mayor of Casterbridge*. Yet the
victim of fate, Henchard, is also the greatest offender against
morality, which would indicate purpose in the suffering he
endures. Moreover, the novel ends on a note of hope because of
Henchard's strength of will and his determination to undergo
suffering and deprivation in order to expiate his sins. It is this
element which makes the book a unique outgrowth of Hardy's
philosophy.

Whether or not Hardy's pessimism seems valid, one should
remember that during his lifetime, Darwin's *The Origin of
Species* undermined the prevailing concept of the divine descent
of man; the "higher criticism" recreated Biblical figures as
humans, not divinities; science reversed prevailing opinions and
superstitions; and life in general grew faster, harsher, less con-

cerned with beauty and art, and more preoccupied with practical economics. Hardy, as a product of his age, was profoundly affected by the violent changes and forces which seemed to toss man about like a rag doll. It was natural that the events of his age should have created in him a deep pessimism, but it was also an exemplary virtue of his spirit that in one of his finest works, *The Mayor of Casterbridge,* he posed the solution of the dilemma: man will overcome because he has the nobility and strength to endure.

Brief Summary of the Novel

In a fit of drunken irritation, Michael Henchard, a young, unemployed hay-trusser, sells his wife Susan and his infant daughter Elizabeth-Jane to a sailor during a fair in the village of Weydon-Priors. Eighteen years later, Susan and Elizabeth-Jane return to seek him out but are told by the "furmity woman," the old hag whose concoction had made Henchard drunk at the fair, that he has moved to the distant town of Casterbridge. The sailor has been reported lost at sea.

Susan and Elizabeth-Jane, the latter innocent of the shameful sale eighteen years before, reach Casterbridge, where they discover that Henchard has become the mayor and one of the wealthiest businessmen in the area. Henchard, out of a sense of guilt, courts Susan in a respectable manner and soon after remarries her, hoping that one day he will be able to acknowledge Elizabeth-Jane as his daughter.

Concurrently with Susan's return, Henchard hires Donald Farfrae, a young Scotsman, as his business manager. After a short while, Susan dies, and Henchard learns that his own daughter had died many years earlier and that Elizabeth-Jane is really the illegitimate daughter of Newson, the sailor, Susan's second "husband."

Lucetta Templeman, a young woman from Jersey with whom Henchard has had a romantic involvement, comes to Casterbridge with the intention of marrying Henchard. She meets Farfrae, however, and the two are deeply attracted. Henchard, deeply disturbed by Farfrae's prestige in the town, has dismissed him, and Farfrae sets up his own rival business. Shortly after, Farfrae and Lucetta are married.

Henchard's fortunes continue their decline while Farfrae's

advance. When Henchard's successor as mayor dies suddenly, Farfrae becomes Mayor. Henchard's ruin is almost completed when the "furmity woman" is arrested as a vagrant in Casterbridge and reveals the transaction two decades earlier when Henchard sold his wife. Then, by a combination of bad luck and mismanagement, Henchard goes bankrupt and is forced to make his living as an employee of Farfrae's.

Lucetta, now at the height of her fortunes, has staked everything on keeping her past relationship with Henchard a secret. Her old love letters to him, however, find their way into the hands of Henchard's vengeful ex-employee, Jopp, who reveals them to the worst element in the town. They organize a "skimmity ride," in which Henchard and Lucetta are paraded in effigy through the streets. The shock of the scandal kills Lucetta.

Now an almost broken man, Henchard moves to the poorest quarters, where his life is made tolerable only by Elizabeth-Jane's kindness and concern. Even his comfort in her affection is threatened, however, when Newson, the sailor, returns in search of his daughter. Henchard's lie to Newson that Elizabeth-Jane has died is eventually discovered, and Elizabeth-Jane, his last source of comfort, turns against him.

Farfrae, after a period as a widower, renews his interest in Elizabeth-Jane. They are married and Henchard, when he comes to deliver a wedding gift, finds Newson enjoying his position as the bride's father. Heartbroken, Henchard leaves and shortly afterwards dies in an abandoned hut, attended only by the humblest and simplest of his former workmen. The novel closes when Farfrae and Elizabeth-Jane find the place where he has died and read his terrible will of complete renunciation.

CHAPTER 1

SYNOPSIS: A WIFE IS SOLD

Michael Henchard, an unemployed hay-trusser "of fine figure, swarthy and stern in aspect," his wife Susan, and their little child Elizabeth-Jane are wearily approaching the Wessex village of Weydon-Priors at the end of a late-summer day in the year 1826. When she looks at the child, Susan is pretty, but her face often has "the hard, half-apathetic expression" of one who expects the worst. They learn from a passer-by that there is no employment in the village. A fair is still in progress, and once the trio has arrived Michael attempts to enter a refreshment tent which advertises "Good Home-brewed Beer, Ale, and Cyder." However, Susan persuades him to enter the booth where "furmity" is sold, since the food is nourishing even if repulsive in appearance.

In the tent Michael pays the furmity woman, "a haggish creature of about fifty," to spike his basin of furmity with large dosages of rum. He quickly finishes a number of well-laced portions and, in a "quarrelsome" mood, begins to bewail the fact that he has ruined his life by marrying too young.

As the liquor takes hold, Michael offers his young wife for sale to the highest bidder. Susan, who has experienced his outrageous displays before, swears that if Michael persists, she will take the child and go with the highest bidder. She ignores the advice of "a buxom staylace dealer" and stands up for the bidding. Michael continues the bidding with renewed vigor and raises the price to five guineas for wife and child. The staylace dealer rebukes him to no effect. Before long, a sailor offers to meet Michael's terms. With the appearance of "real cash the jovial frivolity of the scene departed," and the crowd of listeners "waited with parting lips." Michael accepts the sailor's offer, pocketing the money with an air of finality. Susan and Elizabeth-Jane leave with the sailor, but before they depart she turns to Michael and, sobbing bitterly, flings her wedding ring in his face. The staylace vendor says: "I glory in the woman's sperrit." The shocked spectators—who until now had thought it all a joke—quickly depart, leaving Michael to his own conscience. Within a few moments he falls into a drunken slumber. The furmity woman closes up shop, and Michael is left in the dark, snoring loudly.

DISCUSSION

The physical surroundings in this chapter serve to reinforce the dramatic movement of the unpleasant events. The road toward Weydon-Priors is barren, the leaves on the trees are dull green, and powdered dust covers the road and shrubbery. There is no employment in this village, and, as Michael and Susan learn from a passing stranger, "Pulling down is more the nater of Weydon. . . ."

As we gather soon enough, Michael is portrayed as one given over to fits of despondent self-pity, violent outbursts, and irrevocable spur-of-the-moment decisions. Michael has too much of a liking for strong drink: he at first wants to enter the tent where beer and ale are sold; he is not satisfied with one or two bowls of spiked furmity; he becomes boisterous from the effects; after he has sold his wife, he falls into a stupor. Hardy is, of course, showing that at this point the flaw in Michael's character is aggravated by his liking for drink, which leads him to commit an outrageous act that haunts him for years and finally proves to be his downfall.

Why does Susan go with the sailor? First of all, Hardy has shown that the couple's marital relationship is not healthy, and from his opening descriptions we can easily imagine the silent, endless day's journey passed in an "atmosphere of stale familiarity." Also, it must be remembered that in the early part of the nineteenth century women often had no trades by which they could support themselves in a decent manner. Women were usually completely dependent upon their husbands for their sustenance. Susan realizes all these things. Furthermore, aside from the emotional justification she has for leaving—that is, being sold like a common streetwalker to the highest bidder—she also realizes that Michael has disclaimed all responsibility toward her and the child. Under these circumstances, Susan's choice is understandable.

Hardy lets the reader know in the first sentence that the novel will be laid in Wessex. "Wessex" is an ancient name for the West Saxon kingdom of the Middle Ages, which Hardy revived as a term for the region in which he set most of his novels and stories. (Unlike "Essex," "Sussex," and "Middlesex," it is a term no longer used geographically.) Wessex comprises Dorsetshire and parts of other western English counties, which have a number of local features exploited to great effect by Hardy.

By the time he published *The Mayor of Casterbridge,* Hardy had built a considerable following for his Wessex novels and tales: the reader could expect colorful dialogue, faithfully reproduced; a certain half-humorous, half-crabbed character in the natives; a good deal of poetic treatment of both town and country. The region was large enough not to be too confining for a novelist handling important themes, but small enough to impart color and character to setting.

fustian coarse cotton

thimble-riggers tricksters, conjurers. The expression may refer to the trick of trying to guess under which of three thimbles a pea is hidden. The hand of the "thimble-rigger" was, of course, faster than the eye of the spectator.

Weydon-Priors a village in upper Wessex, probably the fictitious name for Weyhill in northwest Hampshire

begad By God! A slightly toned down oath

'vation salvation

be-right truly; by-right

rheumy sniffling, runny-nose. The word refers to having a cold.

'od shortened from the exclamation, "God!," so as to avoid profanity

keacorn dialect for throat

QUESTION

How do you account for the fact that an incident as improbable-sounding and melodramatic as the sale of a wife seems believable and gripping rather than far-fetched?

CHAPTER 2

SYNOPSIS: THE OATH

Upon awakening the next morning, Michael finds Susan's

wedding ring on the floor and the sailor's money in his pocket. He now understands that the preceding night's events are not a dream, and "in silent thought" walks away from the village into the country. At first he wonders if his name is known.

He is angry with Susan, but, as the consequences of his conduct become clearer, he realizes that Susan's simplicity of mind and sober character will require her to live up to the bargain. He recalls her previous threat to take him at his word. He decides to search for his wife and child and, when he finds them, try to live with his shame. But first he goes to a church and swears an oath before the altar that he will not touch strong drink "for the space of twenty-one years—a year for every year that I have lived." He begins the search for his wife and child, but no one has any recollection of having seen them. His search lasts for months until, having carried his quest to a seaport, he learns that "persons answering somewhat to his description had emigrated a little time before." He abandons his search and journeys southwestward, not stopping until he reaches the town of Casterbridge in a distant part of Wessex.

DISCUSSION

Michael's pride and determination are shown in this chapter. He is willing to search for his wife and live with the shame he has brought upon himself, but his pride will not let him reveal that shame to others, even though such a revelation would certainly help him in his quest. Furthermore, he feels relief that he did not state his name during the transaction. His vow to stop drinking arouses our interest in his future conduct.

It is interesting that Hardy says of Henchard: "there was something fetichistic in this man's beliefs." Hardy has often been accused of fetichism, in the sense of not being satisfied with scientific explanations. The conflict between Hardy's verbal acceptance of the scientific attitude and his love of the supernatural is discussed by Baker, pp. 25–26. (See bibliography.)

With this chapter we reach the end of what is, in effect, the prelude to the major story of *The Mayor of Casterbridge*. As in the prologue to a Greek drama, and in the first scene or two of modern plays, the seeds of the dramatic conflict to follow are planted, and their growth is now about to be witnessed.

"the Seven Sleepers had a dog" referring to a portion found in the *Koran:* Seven sleepers in a **strook**	cave, and their dog the eighth **sacrarium** the sanctuary, or the place before the altar struck

QUESTION

Does Henchard's failure to find his wife suggest that the sale of his wife is a closed chapter or will diminish in importance?

CHAPTER 3

SYNOPSIS: SUSAN AND ELIZABETH-JANE EIGHTEEN YEARS AFTER

It is approximately eighteen years later. Susan Henchard, her face less round and her hair thinner, who now calls herself "Mrs. Newson," is again walking along the dusty road into Weydon-Priors. She walks hand in hand with her daughter, Elizabeth-Jane, young, "well-formed," pretty, and vivacious. The two women are dressed in black, and we learn that Richard Newson, Susan's "husband" who bought her many years ago, has been lost at sea. "Mrs. Newson" is in quest of a "relation," as she has told Elizabeth-Jane, whose name is Michael Henchard, whom she had last seen at the fair in Weydon-Priors. However, she has not told Elizabeth-Jane of her true relationship to Henchard, the hay-trusser.

On the fairgrounds, whose trade has considerably diminished with the passage of time, Susan comes upon the "furmity woman." The furmity woman, now an old crone "tentless" and "dirty," barely able to make a living, does not recognize Susan. Over Elizabeth-Jane's protest, Susan asks her about Michael Henchard. At first the hag does not recollect the shameful event. However, upon reflection she recalls that a man who had figured in such an event had returned about a year after the sale. He left word with her that if a woman were to ask for him, the furmity woman should tell her that he has gone to Casterbridge. Elizabeth-Jane and Susan find lodging for the night before setting out for Casterbridge.

DISCUSSION

This short chapter, which depicts Susan's determination to locate her real husband, serves to explain the long passage of time and to raise two rather interesting problems. There must be a definite need for Susan to find Henchard, else under the circumstances she would never want to see him again. Also, we wonder what kind of complication will arise if she does find him. Perhaps he has remarried.

Elizabeth-Jane says to her mother: "Don't speak to her— it isn't respectable!" when Susan approaches the furmity woman, Mrs. Goodenough. This would indicate that Elizabeth-Jane might be excessively concerned about propriety.

QUESTION

Does Susan's rather uninteresting character lead you to expect exciting developments if she does find Henchard?

CHAPTER 4

SYNOPSIS: HENCHARD'S NAME IS OVERHEARD

A flashback reveals the events of Susan's life as Mrs. Newson. "A hundred times she had been upon the point of telling" Elizabeth-Jane about the past, but it had become "too fearful a thing to contemplate." We learn that the family had emigrated to Canada. We also see that during the eighteen years of their "marriage," Susan's simple nature was manifested by her absolute belief that their relationship was legal and binding. Thus, she and her new husband dwelled together humbly and peacefully for about twelve years in Canada. When Elizabeth-Jane was about twelve, the family returned to England and took up residence at Falmouth, a fishing town in South Cornwall. For a time Newson worked on the docks; he then acquired work in the Newfoundland trade which caused him to make seasonal trips at sea.

Susan's peace of mind is destroyed when, after confiding in a friend, she learns that her relationship with Newson is not a valid one. She finally tells him that their relationship cannot be maintained. The next season Newson is reported lost during a trip to Newfoundland. This news, though painful, is almost a relief to Susan.

Because she has seen Elizabeth-Jane's desire to learn and advance herself, Susan decides to seek out Henchard's help. She fears that without aid the girl, who has "the raw materials of beauty" and a fine mind, will be ruined by endless years of poverty.

Having arrived at Casterbridge, the women hear Henchard's name mentioned by two passing men, but Susan persuades her daughter not to seek him out—"He may be in the workhouse, or in the stocks . . ." They also learn from a gossip that the agricultural town is suffering from a shortage of decent bread, since the "corn-factor" had sold poor wheat to the millers and bakers.

DISCUSSION

This chapter, by means of flashback, brings us up-to-date concerning the intervening years of Susan and Elizabeth-Jane's lives. It also reinforces our understanding of Susan's naive belief in the validity of her second "marriage." Furthermore, we are shown that Elizabeth-Jane is endowed with beauty and intelligence, and that for the encouragement of her daughter's promise only is Susan willing to seek Henchard's aid. Hardy heightens suspense by having Henchard's name mentioned but without the disclosure of details.

Hardy's intimate knowledge of Dorchester (the town after which Casterbridge is modeled) is revealed in the highly detailed description of its streets and layout, its proximity to the countryside, and "the agricultural and pastoral character of the people." His use of concrete detail is a constant feature of Hardy's realism, contributing greatly to his wonderful "atmosphere," although it is sometimes excessive, in the critic Robert B. Heilman's view.

carkings disturbing, worrisome, vexing. This usage is archaic.
butter-firkins a firkin is a wooden vessel for holding butter or lard. Its capacity is usually the equivalent of one-fourth of a barrel.

A butter-firkin is also termed as a unit of measurement approximating 55 or 56 pounds.
seed-lips baskets for seeds
manna-food the food which God supplied to the Children of

Israel during their wanderings in the desert

swipes weak beer

growed wheat underdeveloped, poor wheat which looks developed to the untrained eye

plim blown up, swollen

corn-factor a factor is a commission merchant. In Scotland the meaning may be applied to a managing agent of an estate.

QUESTION

How would you compare Elizabeth-Jane with Susan from the standpoint of interest and dramatic potential?

CHAPTER 5

SYNOPSIS: THE MAYOR OF CASTERBRIDGE

The town band is playing merrily in front of the King's Arms, Casterbridge's chief hotel. A dinner is being held inside for all the town dignitaries and well-to-do citizens, although the windows are left open so the lesser folk can hear. Susan and Elizabeth-Jane are attracted to the gathering in front of the hotel. There they learn that Michael Henchard is the Mayor of Casterbridge. At forty, he is a dynamic, commanding figure, with "a rich complexion, . . . a flashing black eye, and dark, bushy brows and hair." A townsman among the group of spectators informs them that Henchard is also a wealthy businessman, the corn-factor who had sold bad wheat. A surprising note is interjected when the news is given that the Mayor is a complete teetotaler. Rumor has it that a long time ago the Mayor took a "gospel oath" to abstain from alcoholic beverages for many years, and that only two years remain until the oath expires. He gives the impression of a man with "no pity for weakness."

Elizabeth-Jane is eager and excited at learning of the prosperity and high status of her "relation," but Susan is despondent and frightened of meeting Henchard. Elizabeth-Jane discovers by talking to a few villagers that Henchard is thought to be a widower. The feast proceeds merrily inside the hotel until a member of a group of lesser merchants sitting at the farther end of the room asks if Henchard will replace the poor wheat he has sold them with wholesome wheat. The query is echoed among the onlookers ouside. Henchard is visibly upset by the demand, and answers: "If anybody will tell me how to turn grown wheat into wholesome wheat I'll take it back with pleasure. But it can't be done." Previous to this Henchard had informed the assembly that he, too, had been taken in when he bought the wheat. In order to minimize the chances of the recurrence of such a mistake, Henchard has advertised for a competent manager of the corn department. The matter is then dropped.

DISCUSSION

It is easy for us to understand Susan's consternation. She does not see in Michael Henchard a kind and forgiving personality. She is intimidated, too, by his power and affluence: "He overpowers me!" And thus she is left in despair.

Hardy introduces two elements of suspense in this chapter. What will happen when Henchard's oath of abstinence expires in two years? And what kind of manager will he hire? As he does so often, Hardy provides a commentary on the action by presenting the talk of the villagers—his "Wessex" types.

In England the term "corn" means wheat. What Americans call corn is termed "maize" by the English.

fall a veil attached to the hat which women wore as a custom of modesty when walking in public

'a he

rummers a tall stemless glass for drinking

"shaken a little to-year" disturbed or bothered this year

list a strip, or streak

QUESTION

Why does it not seem improbable that Henchard, whom we last saw as a drunken, unemployed farm worker, should now be the dominant figure in a prosperous town?

CHAPTER 6

SYNOPSIS: HENCHARD FOLLOWS THE STRANGER

As the festivities proceed within the King's Arms Hotel,

a handsome stranger "of a fair countenance, bright-eyed, and slight in build," stops before the hotel, his attention arrested by the discussion about corn. After hearing Henchard's closing words on the subject, he hastily scribbles a note and instructs a waiter to deliver it to the Mayor. Having also asked the waiter about a less expensive hotel, he immediately leaves for the Three Mariners Inn. During all this time, Elizabeth-Jane has watched the young man's actions, and after his departure suggests to her mother that they, too, look for a lodging at the Three Mariners. Susan agrees and they also leave.

Henchard is given the note and upon reading it becomes evidently interested in its contents. He learns from the waiter that a young Scotsman sent the note and that he has gone to the Three Mariners. Henchard leaves the dinner-party—where most of the members have become tipsy—and walks to the inn.

DISCUSSION

This chapter may be considered as the beginning of the complex plot movements of the novel. It is interesting because a number of chance happenings occur which create the initial impetus of the events to follow: by chance a handsome Scotsman passes by the hotel and hears the discussion concerning corn; Elizabeth-Jane has traveled a great distance to listen to the same discussion and by chance to notice the young Scotsman; the three strangers go to the same inn, and Henchard, leaving the dinner-party to seek out the young Scotsman, by chance just misses his wife and Elizabeth-Jane. *If* Henchard had come upon Susan five minutes earlier, he might never have gone to the Three Mariners and the story would have been drastically altered. But this is only one of many chance "if's" the reader will encounter within the movement of the plot.

The Three Mariners is lovingly described, illustrating Hardy's recurrent fascination with the old, quaint, "native" aspects of Wessex.

mullioned a vertical dividing strip in an opening or a window. The sense of the passage is that the vertical strips on the windows should be perpendicular to the ground, but they are not. Thus, the building looks quaintly out of kilter.

yard of clay a long clay pipe

ruddy polls ruddy—reddish, healthy glow; poll—top or back of the head. Hence, shiny bald heads visible through the shutters of the Inn.

QUESTION

What function does the Three Mariners Inn serve in the story apart from local color?

CHAPTER 7

SYNOPSIS: A CONVERSATION BETWEEN HENCHARD AND FARFRAE IS OVERHEARD

Despite the modesty of their accommodations at the Three Mariners, Susan believes that they are "too good for us." Elizabeth-Jane is pleased at their "respectability," however. Unknown to her mother, she offers to defray some of the expense by working as a servingmaid in the busy bar. During these duties she is required to bring the young Scotsman's meal to his quarters. She does so, and while serving the meal takes the chance to study his handsome bearing. She also notices that the young man's room is directly beside the one she shares with her mother.

When Elizabeth-Jane finally returns to the room with their own meal, Susan motions her to remain silent. Michael Henchard is in the room next door with the young Scotsman, whose name they learn is Donald Farfrae. Because of the thinness of the walls, their entire conversation is audible next door.

It is learned that Donald Farfrae's note to Henchard contained information on how to restore grown wheat to wholesome second quality. Henchard is sure, as a result, that the young man is the one who answered his advertisement for a corn-manager, but Farfrae assures him that is not so. Farfrae, being kind and generous, demonstrates the procedure to Henchard free-of-charge. Henchard is astounded by Farfrae's ability and immediately offers him the position of corn-manager, plus a commission. However, Farfrae is just passing through on his way to Bristol where he plans to take ship to the New World: "I wish I could stay—sincerely I would like to," he replied. "But no—it cannet be! . . . I want to see the warrld." Showing bitter disappointment, Henchard must make do with this

reply despite his liberal offer and persistent pleas. Farfrae offers
Henchard a glass of ale, which is refused. Henchard states his
reason for refusing: "When I was a young man I went in for
that sort of thing too strong—far too strong—and was well-
nigh ruined by it! I did a deed on account of it which I shall
be ashamed of to my dying day."

DISCUSSION

We see that Henchard is a lonely man and has been looking for another employee who would be of value to him in his
business and as a friend. Hardy is careful to convince the reader
of Henchard's friendly attraction to the younger man who is
temperamentally and physically the opposite of Henchard. We
also see that Henchard is continually hounded by his youthful
deed. There is a hint that Henchard is still the same, however,
in the ease with which he forgets the prior claim to the corn-
manager's job of the applicant named "Jipp" or "Jopp."

QUESTION

What is the importance of Henchard's offering the corn-
manager's job to a man who is not the one expecting it?

CHAPTER 8

SYNOPSIS: FARFRAE SINGS AT THE
THREE MARINERS

Elizabeth-Jane goes to remove Farfrae's supper tray, leaving Susan in their room, her face "strangely bright since Henchard's avowal of shame." Farfrae joins the patrons on the
ground floor of the Three Mariners and before long is charming
them with a plaintive Scotch ballad. Elizabeth-Jane, having
cleared away Farfrae's dinner dishes, as well as her own,
watches Donald from an inconspicuous spot. Farfrae is engaged
in conversation by the townspeople, and because of his own
trusting and higher nature refuses to accept the townspeople's
belittling of Casterbridge. By popular acclaim he is required to
sing some more songs, after which he takes his leave to retire.

Elizabeth-Jane, who has just turned down Farfrae's bedding upon the request of the landlady, passes him on the stairs. She is embarrassed and does not look at him. Farfrae, however, is drawn to her and sings a ditty apparently intended for her.

Before retiring, Elizabeth-Jane tells her mother about Farfrae. It is obvious that the similar, serious nature of their characters appeals to her and that she is attracted to him. When Susan speaks of Henchard as "he," Elizabeth-Jane assumes that "he" is Farfrae.

Outside the inn Henchard paces back and forth, disturbed because Farfrae has rejected his offer. He hears Farfrae's singing and says to himself: "To be sure, to be sure, how that fellow does draw me, . . . I suppose 'tis because I'm so lonely. I'd have given him a third share in the business to have stayed!"

DISCUSSION

Farfrae shows himself to be an appealing and charming young man. The townspeople take to him immediately since he is a man of creative ability as well as charm, and such men are not to be found in Casterbridge. Also, the scene between Elizabeth-Jane and Farfrae, though still strangers, serves the purpose of showing them drawing ever closer. Henchard's remarks, on the other hand, display his interest in Farfrae and foreshadow his reliance upon him in personal and business matters.

The scene in the inn is again a distinctively Hardyan touch of Wessex local color. The charm of the rustics comes through in their dialect and poetic speech-rhythms, but there is an undertone of sourness and ill humor in these characters also.

danged damned (used as an expletive)

lammigers lame people

wheel ventilator a fan which revolves by the action of the wind

Gallows Hill a reference to the English Civil War incident in the seventeenth century which resulted in the sentencing to death of about 300 people

ballet ballad

bruckle not trustworthy

Botany Bay penal colony in Australia

chiney china, dishes

chine a ridge or strip of wood; refers to such a strip on the bottom of a cask, on which the workman turns the cask, thus moving it without tipping it over

gaberlunzie wandering beggar

QUESTION

Does Farfrae's immediate popularity among the townspeople hint at anything that might develop later in the story?

CHAPTER 9

SYNOPSIS: FARFRAE TAKES THE JOB

The next morning, Donald Farfrae meets Henchard and together they walk to the end of town. Elizabeth-Jane sees the two men walking away and is sad and hurt at Donald's departure—he has seen her but has neither spoken nor smiled. Susan, bolstered by Henchard's quickness to like a complete stranger, his loneliness, and his avowed shame for his past behavior, sends Elizabeth-Jane to him with a note. Elizabeth-Jane is told to introduce herself and inform Henchard that a distant relative of his—her mother, the widow of a sailor—has arrived in Casterbridge. Elizabeth-Jane is instructed to bring back word when Henchard will meet with Susan. If Henchard refuses to see her, Susan and Elizabeth-Jane will leave town immediately.

As she walks to Henchard's place of business, Elizabeth-Jane is introduced to the bustling life of early morning Casterbridge. When she finally enters Henchard's business office she is shocked speechless to see Donald Farfrae at work. Donald does not seem to recognize her and tells her that Mr. Henchard is busy but will be with her soon. We learn from a brief flashback that Farfrae has accepted Henchard's last-minute, urgent plea to stay and name his own price.

DISCUSSION

A number of relevant incidents occur in this chapter. By sending Elizabeth-Jane to Henchard, Susan begins a restoration of her former relationship with Henchard. Elizabeth-Jane, in order to get to Henchard's place of business, must take a short walk through the town. Thus the reader is given a tour of the quaint surroundings and bustling commercial life of the town, and remains aware that Henchard is at the top of the seemingly endless business activity. Finally, Farfrae is persuaded to stay, and the hint of a relationship between him and Elizabeth-Jane is given.

Suspense is also created when the author deftly interposes the walk through the town to mask the discussion between Henchard and Farfrae and delay the actual meeting between Henchard and Elizabeth-Jane.

Hardy is almost lyrical in his appreciation of Casterbridge on market-day, when its closeness to the country is most pronounced, "differing from the many manufacturing towns which are as foreign bodies set down . . . in a green world with which they have nothing in common."

kerb curb

chassez-déchassez *chassé,* a quick set of gliding, sideward movements in dancing, always led by the same foot; from the French, *chasser.* Hence, *chassez-déchassez,* a French dance from right to left

terpsichorean figures Terpsichore, Greek Muse of the dance; figures in dance positions

netting fish-seines making fishing nets; also, fixing or repairing the nets

amaze amazement

Flemish ladders ladders whose sides become narrower toward the top

staddles a raised frame, or a platform used for stacking hay or straw to avoid contamination from moisture or vermin

QUESTION

Why has the question of Farfrae's employment suddenly assumed an importance equal to that of Susan's quest for Henchard?

CHAPTER 10

SYNOPSIS: HENCHARD "BUYS SUSAN BACK"

While Elizabeth-Jane is waiting for Henchard, Joshua Jopp, the applicant for the position of manager of the corn department, arrives as Henchard enters the room. Henchard informs him abruptly that the position is filled and dismisses him. Jopp leaves, "his mouth twitched with anger, and . . . bitter disappointment . . . written in his face everywhere."

Elizabeth-Jane reveals herself as the daughter of his "relative," Susan, to Henchard, who is shocked. He understands when Elizabeth-Jane refers to her family name as "Newson" that Susan has not revealed the truth to her child. They go indoors and after a few questions concerning the newcomer's past life, Henchard writes a note to Susan and places five guineas in it. He is visibly moved by Elizabeth-Jane's appearance and instructs her to deliver the note personally. Elizabeth-Jane leaves, touched by Henchard's concern. Henchard suddenly suspects that the pair might be impostors, but quickly changes his mind when he reflects upon Elizabeth-Jane's demeanor.

Upon her return Elizabeth-Jane is required to describe to her mother in explicit detail the meeting with Henchard. Susan reads the note which instructs her to tell Elizabeth-Jane nothing and to meet him at eight o'clock that night at the Ring on the Budmouth road. She finds the five guineas enclosed, and though nothing was said of the money in the note, the amount would suggest that Henchard was buying her back again.

DISCUSSION

The suspense of the last chapter is relieved by Henchard's kind treatment of Elizabeth-Jane. It is also significant to Susan that Henchard has enclosed five guineas in the note, the same amount which he received from Newson. He is, in effect, symbolically buying her back.

However, two elements of suspense enter the story here. Note that Henchard has created a potential enemy by his abrupt treatment of Joshua Jopp. Also, frightened of the shame which could be heaped upon him if the truth were known, Henchard arranges a secret meeting with Susan that night in a lonely spot outside of town. This is the beginning of the secretiveness that will surround their reunion. As will be seen in the next chapter, the place of the meeting will significantly add to the mystery.

Henchard's tactfulness in asking about Susan's poverty is in character. Several times in the novel he shows great consideration for people who are in need.

rouge-et-noir from the French: red and black. See the previous description of Henchard as Elizabeth-Jane entered Henchard's office.

Family Bible, *Josephus*, *Whole Duty of Man* three works considered indispensable in every respectable household. The Family Bible was a large Bible which usually contained a page in the front for recording marriages, births, deaths; Josephus Flavius (A.D. 37–100?), Jewish historian and statesman. His *History of the Jewish War* and other work shed much valuable light upon the occurrences of the Bible; *Whole Duty of Man*, 1658, of anonymous origin. A book of devotions.

QUESTION

What clues as to future developments can you perceive in Henchard's brief note?

CHAPTER 11

SYNOPSIS: A MEETING AT THE RING

Henchard meets Susan in the ruins of an old Roman amphitheatre outside of town. The amphitheatre is very large and dark, and due to the gloomy superstitions connected with its grim history almost no one comes there except for "appointments of a furtive kind." It is for this reason—so no one will know of his meeting with Susan—that Henchard arranges for the interview in such a forbidding place as "the Ring."

Henchard's first words to Susan are: "I don't drink, . . . You hear, Susan?—I don't drink now—I haven't since that night." During their discussion, Henchard learns that Susan had considered her alliance with Newson a binding one. She tells Henchard that if she had not thought that way, her life would have been "very wicked." Henchard says that he knows this and feels her to be an "innocent woman." He proposes that she and Elizabeth-Jane rent a house on High Street; after a courtship Susan and Michael will be remarried.

It is most important to Henchard that Elizabeth-Jane remain in complete ignorance of the past. When Susan and Henchard are remarried, Elizabeth-Jane will live with them as Henchard's step-daughter. He considers this to be the best way of fooling the town. Of course he will pay all their expenses. Susan agrees. As she is leaving, Henchard asks: "But just one word. Do you forgive me, Susan?" Susan murmurs something indistinctly and Henchard replies: "Never mind—all in good time, . . . Judge me by my future works—good-bye!"

DISCUSSION

Hardy takes great care in describing the Roman amphitheatre and its unsavory history. He certainly does want the reader to feel the darkness and the gloom of the surroundings in order to emphasize the mystery of the events. Such melancholy settings are common in Hardy's work, and serve to underscore his fancy for the grotesque. This particular setting also reveals his awareness of the Roman element in Wessex.

As Susan leaves, it appears that Henchard has indeed repented and that all will soon be well.

the Ring referring to Maumbury Rings in Dorchester, which served as the public gallows for the first half of the 18th century. Its history goes back many centuries. Under the Romans it was an arena for gladiatorial and wild beast displays. There is a certain unwholesome aura surrounding the Ring due to its history.

Jotuns giants in Norse mythology

rub o't rub of it: a problem, hindrance, doubt

aeolian modulations Aeolus, in Greek mythology, was god of the winds. The aeolian harp was a stringed instrument constructed to produce musical sounds when exposed to the action of the wind.

***must* start genteel** must begin in a manner appropriate to a well-bred person

QUESTION

Does Henchard's plan for "courting" Susan again seem to you as "natural and easy" as he says?

CHAPTER 12

SYNOPSIS: HENCHARD TELLS FARFRAE OF HIS PAST

Henchard returns home to find Donald Farfrae working late over the books. He brings Donald into his home and they have dinner together. After dinner, as they sit beside the fire, Henchard reveals his past to his new-found friend. Donald agrees that Henchard should try to make amends to Susan. However, Henchard further reveals that during his years as a lonely "widower" he had established a relationship with a young woman on the island of Jersey, who had once nursed him through a long illness. Their affair had become known, causing the young woman to suffer much from the scandal. Henchard, after hearing of her sufferings in her letters, proposed marriage to her if she would take the chance that Susan would not return. She readily agreed to this, but now Henchard realizes that his first duty is to Susan and that he cannot marry the other woman. Because she is in bad financial straits, he wishes to help her as best he can. Donald agrees to write a kindly letter to the young lady since Henchard would probably do a bad job of it. Yet Donald thinks that Henchard should tell Elizabeth-Jane that she is his daughter; Henchard cannot agree to that. Henchard mails the letter with a check, and as he returns home speaks aloud to himself: "Can it be that it will go off so easily! . . . Poor thing—God knows! Now then, to make amends to Susan!"

DISCUSSION

Hardy remains true to the character he has established for Henchard. Henchard is still the mercurial man he always was. He has known Donald Farfrae for only one day, yet he tells him what he has told no other living man. Henchard rationalizes that he is lonely. Since Donald is the only man he is genuinely fond of, it is fitting that he reveal himself to his friend. The reader knows, though, that it is really Henchard's characteristic spur-of-the-moment trait that causes him to talk of his past. Farfrae changes his plan to eat alone "gracefully," but he has already seen that Henchard's impulsiveness can mean inconvenience.

With the introduction of the young woman in Jersey, a new complication is brought into the story. Indeed, the mere fact that Henchard confides in Farfrae is another plot twist which at first does not seem too important. Hardy does not attempt to show the reunion with Susan in an optimistic light. Even Henchard's last remarks foreshadow some difficulties.

espaliers trellises or stakes on which small fruit trees or plants are trained to grow in a flattened-out state

"like Job, I could curse the day that gave me birth." from the *Book of Job,* in which Job, in the midst of his suffering, actually curses the day of his birth

sequestrated taken over for the purpose of settling claims

mun Scotch and British dialect: must

QUESTION

What implications do you detect in Henchard's revelation to Farfrae that he has had an affair with a young woman on the island of Jersey?

CHAPTER 13

SYNOPSIS: THE "MARRIAGE"

Michael Henchard installs Susan and Elizabeth-Jane in a cottage located in the western part of Casterbridge. The cottage is pleasant and well furnished. Henchard has even acquired a servant for Susan, to help create an aura of respectability.

As soon as Elizabeth-Jane and Susan are established in the cottage, Henchard calls upon them and stays for tea. Henchard pursues his courtship for a respectable period of time. It gives him some pleasure that Elizabeth-Jane has accepted the events and knows nothing of the truth, but Susan feels regretful at having deceived her child. One day Henchard asks Susan to name the day of their marriage. Susan fears that she is causing him too much trouble. Indeed, she had never planned on anything so elaborate as a remarriage. Henchard is resolved to make amends to Susan, provide a comfortable home for Elizabeth-Jane, and demean himself by marrying a woman who in the eyes of the town would seem to be beneath his status. He tells her that since he has acquired an excellent new business manager, he will have more time to devote to his family in the future.

The townspeople begin to talk about the upcoming marriage, and "Mrs. Newson" is nicknamed "The Ghost," because of her fragile, pale appearance. On a drizzly day in November, Susan and Henchard are remarried. The townspeople waiting outside the church comment upon Henchard's foolishness in marrying a woman so far beneath him. Christopher Coney makes a remark typical of the town's feelings: " 'Tis five-and-forty years since I had my settlement in this here town," said Coney; "but daze me if ever I see a man wait so long before to take so little!" He and the other rustics expatiate humorously on the disparity.

DISCUSSION

The culmination of Henchard's dogged attempts to make amends to Susan is realized in their marriage. However, the chapter is written to give the reader a feeling of malaise. Susan does not think it at all humorous that Elizabeth-Jane has been deceived by them, and in her futile way almost asks Henchard to drop the idea of marriage. However, because Henchard is still a man of stubborn will, he insists upon going through with it. The rain adds to the oppressiveness.

The townspeople also help to give the reader a sense of uneasiness about the proceedings. It has to be admitted that Hardy may be exaggerating somewhat the townspeople's ability to observe so much of hidden history from the appearance of the couple, but the mere mention of the word "bluebeardy" with its associations of cruelty and ruthlessness is enough to create the feeling of impending trouble.

There is a good deal of Hardy's earthy poetry in the villagers' comments. The reader will appreciate the author's artfulness by reading some of this aloud, especially Mrs. Cuxsom's wonderful passage, beginning: "And dostn't mind how mother would sing."

'en   dialect for "him"
zilver-snuffers   silver snuffers; a snuffer is a scissors-like instrument used for clipping the wick of a candle
cow-barton   a cow-yard
"She'll wish her cake dough . . ."   She'll wish she hadn't done it

twanking   whining; in this sense weak and helpless
jumps or night-rail   jumps would be equal to corset-stays, and a night-rail equivalent to a nightgown
small table ninepenny   cheap drinks

QUESTION

Is Nance Mockridge's remark about Susan, "She'll wish her cake dough afore she's done of him," just village chatter?

CHAPTER 14

SYNOPSIS: ELIZABETH-JANE AND FARFRAE ARE BROUGHT TOGETHER

Susan and Elizabeth-Jane fit almost inconspicuously into Henchard's large house. Henchard is most kind to Susan, and her life begins to acquire the melancholy contentment of a late Indian summer. Elizabeth-Jane, however, finds her life growing more and more pleasurable. She no longer suffers from economic distress, and all that she sees is hers for the asking. But, due to

her serious nature, Elizabeth-Jane does not allow her newly acquired position to alter her sober tastes and thoughtful respectability. Moreover, she still has "that field-mouse fear of the
coulter of destiny," believing it would be "tempting Provi-
dence" if she were "too gay." As times passes, she begins to
develop into a physically mature and beautiful young lady.

Henchard notices Elizabeth-Jane's light hair and asks Susan
if she hadn't once assured him that it would become dark.
Alarmed, Susan jerks his foot, and he admits to having nearly
disclosed their secret.

One day Henchard asks Susan if Elizabeth-Jane, of whom
he has grown extremely fond, would consider changing her
name to Henchard. Susan seems reluctant to allow it, but sub-
mits to his will and informs Elizabeth-Jane. Henchard tells
Elizabeth-Jane that she need not change her name from Newson
to Henchard to please him only. Upon hearing this from
Henchard, Elizabeth-Jane decides to retain her own name and
nothing more is said of the matter.

Elizabeth-Jane notices that Henchard has a great deal of
affection and respect for Donald Farfrae, and is seen with him
continually. Farfrae's quiet humor sometimes arouses "a perfect
cannonade of laughter" from Henchard. Under Farfrae's expert
guidance, Henchard's business is modernized in accordance with
the finest business procedures and thrives most successfully.
Farfrae begins to find Henchard's "tigerish affection" a bit confining and suggests that his use as "a second pair of eyes" is
being wasted if both employer and employee are always in the
same place. Henchard explosively rejects the idea.

One day Elizabeth-Jane receives a note requesting her to
come immediately to a granary on Durnover Hill. She goes
there and, as she is waiting, Donald Farfrae arrives. Too shy
to meet him there alone, Elizabeth-Jane hides. As the rain falls,
Donald waits patiently until Elizabeth-Jane reveals her presence
by accidentally dislodging some wheat husks. After Donald
acknowledges her presence, they both realize that someone else
has sent them the identical letter. Donald believes that someone
has played a trick upon them and that Elizabeth-Jane should not
mention it in the future. He helps her remove the wheat husks
from her clothing before she departs. It is obvious that he is
affected by her beauty.

DISCUSSION

A number of hints are scattered throughout this chapter that something unexpected may occur. Henchard distinctly remembers that Elizabeth-Jane's hair promised to be black when she was a child. Susan, of course, informs him that it is natural for the color to change with maturity. Susan is also reluctant to agree to Henchard's request that Elizabeth-Jane change her name to his. Furthermore, we find that Henchard is growing ever more fond of Elizabeth-Jane. With the trick played on Donald and Elizabeth-Jane—which results in Donald's acquiring an added interest in Elizabeth-Jane—it becomes obvious that fate, or someone, wants to bring them together.

Donald's mild chafing at Henchard's possessiveness, and the latter's continued "poor opinion" of Donald's physical smallness also hint at possible conflicts to come.

Martinmas summer late or Indian summer; that is, Susan's life became more bearable in her later years

spencer a bodice

viva voce by voice, oral; that is, Henchard kept almost no business books or records (Italian)

winnowing machine a machine used to separate grain from the chaff

victorine a scarf worn over neck and shoulders

QUESTION

Who do you think is the author of the notes?

CHAPTER 15

SYNOPSIS: HENCHARD AND DONALD QUARREL

Elizabeth-Jane begins experimenting with fine clothing and before long realizes that she is considered the town beauty. Donald Farfrae becomes even more interested in her as time passes. She balances her exhilaration by reflecting sadly on her own intellectual shortcomings.

One morning, vexed out of all patience by the continual tardiness of Abel Whittle, one of his workers, Henchard goes to Whittle's cottage, routs him out of bed, and forces him to go to work without his britches. Whittle is mortified but must go through with it since he needs the employment. Donald sees the embarrassing spectacle, reverses Henchard's orders, and tells Whittle to go home and get his britches. When Henchard hears of this, he and Donald quarrel in front of the men. Donald threatens to quit but gets his way.

As time goes by, Henchard is bothered by Farfrae's popularity among the workers and townspeople. He learns one day from a boy that the people prefer Farfrae's business judgment to his own and consider Donald his superior in every way. While going to estimate the value of some hay, Henchard meets Donald, who has been summoned to the same task. Henchard accuses Donald of indiscriminately hurting his feelings. Donald sincerely denies that such a thing could be. Henchard parts from his friend on good terms once again, but now always thinks of him "with a dim dread."

DISCUSSION

This chapter demonstrates not only Elizabeth-Jane's increasing awareness that she is a mature, beautiful woman but also her essential lack of vanity and giddiness. It also shows that Donald has acquired more than a passing interest in her. (Henchard, of course, does not suspect that Donald secretly admires Elizabeth-Jane.) After the quarrel, Henchard treats Donald more formally, and his overbearing friendship diminishes to a more courteous but distant relationship. As time passes, Henchard regrets having told Donald about his life. His regret is intensified when he learns the townspeople prefer Donald to him. Even though the quarrel is mended, Henchard still feels a "dim dread" concerning Farfrae.

the prophet Baruch   in the *Apocrypha.* The sense is that Elizabeth-Jane was not considered a truly great beauty adulated by all.

Rochefoucauld   French author whose philosophy states that human conduct is motivated by selfishness

fretted my gizzard   worried

diment   diamond

sotto voce   under one's breath, in a low voice (Italian)

scantling   a little bit, a tiny piece

QUESTION

What is the significance of the disclosure that "Henchard had kept Abel's old mother in coals and snuff all the previous winter"?

CHAPTER 16

SYNOPSIS: DONALD'S DISMISSAL

On the occasion of the "celebration of a national event," Donald borrows a number of rick-cloths from Henchard for an entertainment. Spurred on by Donald's initiative, Henchard decides to provide an elaborate outdoor entertainment complete with food and games. He is sure that everyone will come to his festivities since they are free, and Donald plans to "charge admission at the rate of so much a head."

On the day of the holiday a heavy rain ruins the turnout at Henchard's free festivities. He orders the games and tables removed and later goes into Casterbridge where he sees all the people flocking to a dance. Ingeniously, Donald has used the rick-cloths as a large tent between some trees within the town. Henchard hears the gay music and notices the warmth of the surroundings and the abandon of the dancers. Even Susan and Elizabeth-Jane have come to the dance which is, in the eyes of the people, an unqualified success far exceeding the efforts of the Mayor. Donald is the center of the proceedings, and even Elizabeth-Jane dances with him. Henchard overhears the cruel remarks of the townspeople and, goaded by the taunts and jests of other town officials, states that Donald's term as manager is drawing to a close. Donald quietly corroborates the declaration. Henchard goes home that night, satisfied that he is protecting his hard-won reputation. The next morning he deeply regrets his rash statement. He soon becomes aware that Donald plans "to take him at his word."

DISCUSSION

Once again Hardy places the reader within the mind of Henchard. We see the total failure of Henchard's plans, and for a moment it appears that everything is going wrong for him. Through Henchard's eyes we see Donald's unqualified success with the townspeople, and for a fleeting second we feel the jealousy Henchard feels. It is no surprise that Henchard acts the way he does, especially since we have listened with him to the ugly remarks and jests of the townspeople. In this chapter and in Chapter 15, Hardy has cleverly shifted the emphasis away from the Susan-Henchard-Elizabeth-Jane development and concentrated on the Henchard-Farfrae relationship.

Correggio famous Italian artist (1494–1534)

stunpoll stone head

"Miss M'Leod of Ayr" a tune that Hardy knew when a child

skipping on the small skipping in small "skips"

randy Scotch dialect: boisterous, fun-loving. The sense is that

Donald's character is one that loves merry-making, as opposed to Henchard's more staid personality.

"Jack's as good as his master" a proverb. The meaning is that the servant has become as good as the employer.

QUESTION

What do you make of the fact that Farfrae is firmer and more competent than the other victims of Henchard's impulsiveness?

CHAPTER 17

SYNOPSIS: DONALD GOES INTO BUSINESS

Elizabeth-Jane is covered with shame when someone hints that "she had not been quite in her place" in dancing with such pleasure in "a mixed throng." Donald accompanies Elizabeth-Jane to her home after she has left the dance. He reveals the break between Henchard and himself and states that he would ask her something special if only he were richer. Elizabeth-Jane asks him not to leave Casterbridge. She hurries home and thinks intensely about him.

Donald soon makes the break complete by purchasing his own hay and corn business. However, since he feels that Henchard has been very kind to him, he decides not to compete with him commercially. He is sure that there is ample business for both of them. He even turns away his first customer, a man who had dealt with Henchard within the last three months. Henchard now holds no affection for Donald and considers him an enemy, but his abuse of Donald finds little sympathy in the town council. He immediately forbids Elizabeth-Jane to have any further relationship with Donald and in a crisp letter informs Donald of his step-daughter's promise to obey his request.

Donald's business prospers, and though he had not attempted to come into competition with Henchard, he is forced "to close with Henchard in mortal commercial combat" when Henchard begins a price war. Before long, to add to Henchard's bitterness, Donald is given an official business stall at the market. He cannot bear to hear Farfrae's name mentioned at home.

DISCUSSION

This chapter brings the Henchard-Farfrae relationship to a complete break. Though Donald still has friendly feelings toward Henchard, Henchard considers him an enemy and forces him to engage in highly commercial competition. We also see that Henchard's friends and council members are not impressed with his statement that he will meet Donald's competition head-on. Apparently he has caused each one of them some pain in the past. This is probably the strongest hint so far that Henchard's fluctuating temperament has not earned him one friend. There are also two slight hints that Susan had wanted Elizabeth-Jane and Donald to get to know each other better.

This chapter contains the statement: "Character is Fate, said Novalis," one of the most widely discussed comments Hardy ever made in his novels. It appears to conflict with Hardy's emphasis on chance and impersonal forces as factors in man's fate, but it is certainly consistent with the character of Henchard throughout.

voot foot
wo'th a varden worth a farthing
sniff and snaff haven't agreed to more than accepting his gentlemanly attentions (especially in regard to matrimonial plans), would be the sense of the expression
modus vivendi working arrangement; a way of living (Latin)

Novalis Baron Friedrich von Hardenburg (1772–1801) whose pen-name was Novalis; poet and novelist
Faust the main character in Goethe's monumental drama
Bellerophon character in Greek legends who killed his brother and fled from the society of mankind

QUESTION

What is the ethical implication of Hardy's phrase for Henchard as a Faust-like being "who had quitted the ways of vulgar men without light to guide him on a better way"?

CHAPTER 18

SYNOPSIS: SUSAN'S DEATH

Elizabeth-Jane's fears for her mother are confirmed. Susan becomes seriously ill, too weak to leave her room. Henchard gets the town's "richest, busiest doctor," but Elizabeth-Jane now fears the worst.

Henchard receives a letter from Jersey in which the young lady who had nursed him absolves him of any share in her troubles. She asks only that he meet her and return her letters which, though she only hints at it, could be compromising to her one day. The letter is signed, "Lucetta." Henchard brings the letters, but Lucetta does not arrive.

Susan, sensing her imminent death, writes a letter addressed to "Mr. Michael Henchard. Not to be opened till Elizabeth-Jane's wedding-day." As Elizabeth-Jane sits up with her mother one night, Susan confesses that it was she that sent the notes to Donald and her daughter: "It was not to make fools of you—it was done to bring you together. 'Twas I did it. . . . I—wanted you to marry Mr. Farfrae. . . . Well, I had a reason. 'Twill out one day. I wish it could have been in my time! But there—nothing is as you wish it! Henchard hates him."

Susan dies quietly one Sunday morning. The reader learns of her death through Donald's concern.

DISCUSSION

In this chapter Hardy ends Susan's struggle with life. However, he introduces new material which will create suspense and compensate for the loss of one of the characters. Lucetta makes an intriguing entry by sending Henchard a letter, then failing to meet him at the time and place proposed. Susan, prompted by some thought which we as yet do not know, writes a mysterious letter to Henchard with instructions to delay its opening until Elizabeth-Jane's wedding. Furthermore, utilizing Henchard's characteristic practicality, Hardy allows Henchard to think of marrying Lucetta after Susan's death. This is another grotesque touch whose enormity is only surpassed by the discussion of the townspeople at the end of the chapter. The theme of man's inability to cope with arbitrary causes is propounded succinctly as Elizabeth-Jane sits by her mother, ruminating over her own life. Elizabeth-Jane continues to grow in richness of character—she is now "the subtle-souled girl."

The village characters, despite their ghoulish humors, add interest and amusement with their running commentary in Hardy's unique rustic style.

doxology the character means "theology," but even then 'theology" would not be the appropriate word.

varnished for 'natomies skeleton bones sold, varnished, and used in colleges or schools for the study of anatomy

QUESTION

What can you tell about Lucetta's character from the style and content of her letter to Henchard?

CHAPTER 19

SYNOPSIS: HENCHARD READS SUSAN'S LETTER

Three weeks after Susan's funeral, prompted by loneliness and bothered by Elizabeth-Jane's inability to accept him as her father, Henchard impulsively reveals to Elizabeth-Jane that he is her real father. However, he hides from her the complete truth by telling her that Susan had thought him dead and had remarried. Elizabeth-Jane is confused at first. Henchard asks her if she will now consent to change her name to his. She agrees, and the letter is written and sent to the *Casterbridge Chronicle*. Henchard leaves her to find documentary proof of his marriage to Susan, but as he is rummaging through his papers, Susan's poorly sealed letter falls open before him. He reads the letter. It is Susan's revelations that Elizabeth-Jane is *not* his child, but Newson's. Henchard's little girl had died three months after he sold his wife.

Henchard's plans for happiness are now blasted. All that night he walks alone through the dismal northeastern part of town, where the jail and gallows are, meditating on the fate he has brought upon himself. He feels that he must continue along the path he has started rather than face abiding humiliation. When he greets Elizabeth-Jane at breakfast, she tells him that she has accepted him as her true father. But there is no joy for him in these long-awaited words: "His reinstation of her mother had been chiefly for the girl's sake, and the fruition of the whole scheme was such dust and ashes as this."

DISCUSSION

Fate seems to be closing in upon Henchard. Everything he does appears to be destined to failure. His elaborate scheme to remarry Susan and regain his child has almost succeeded, but if he had not been prompted by paternal, possessive feelings toward Elizabeth-Jane, he would not have searched for proof to show her. Thus, he would not have found Susan's letter of confession. It becomes apparent even to Henchard that some blind, dooming fate has structured the events of his life in a series of false leads toward happiness, only to dash them at the last moment.

pier-glass mirror
rosette an ornament resembling a badge similar to a rose
Prester John in mythology, a king who was punished by the gods. He was condemned to have his food snatched from him by harpies, half-woman, half-birdlike creatures who acted as the gods' avengers.
Schwarzwasser black-water. It is also the name of a river in Poland. (German)
weir an obstruction or dam placed in a stream to divert or raise the waters

QUESTION

In the light of what you already know about Henchard, how do you expect the revelation in Susan's letter to affect his future attitude toward Elizabeth-Jane?

CHAPTER 20

SYNOPSIS: ELIZABETH-JANE MEETS A CHARMING STRANGER

Henchard becomes cold toward Elizabeth-Jane and critical of her lapses into country dialect, her bold handwriting, and her kindness to servants. His behavior to her worsens when the servant Nance Mockridge defiantly tells him Elizabeth-Jane had once worked as a waitress in a pub. The revelation that she had served at the Three Mariners is a bitter blow, and its bitterness is compounded by the news that he is not going to be chosen as an alderman at the end of his mayoralty, but that Donald Farfrae is to be offered a council seat. He begins to leave Elizabeth-Jane alone most of the time, preferring to have his meals with the farmers at the hotel. Henchard finally realizes that Farfrae could take Elizabeth-Jane off his hands, so he writes a letter to him stating that he may continue his court-ship of Elizabeth-Jane.

Elizabeth-Jane is miserable, "a dumb, deep-feeling, great-eyed creature," and feels that Henchard disdains her because of her lack of education. Unknown to Henchard, she spends her empty hours patiently studying and reading. Between the inter-vals of study she visits her mother's grave. One morning as she stands before her mother's grave she meets a charming lady. The stranger's way are so disarming and sympathetic that Elizabeth-Jane reveals her past and her present unhappiness. The listener is kind, but "her anxiety not to condemn Henchard while siding with Elizabeth" is "curious." The newcomer in-forms Elizabeth-Jane that she will become a resident of Caster-bridge at High-Place Hall and that she would like the unhappy girl to stay with her as a companion. Elizabeth-Jane quickly assents and joyfully contemplates her new position.

DISCUSSION

The plot movement has slowed momentarily, but much attention is given to Henchard's growing dislike of Elizabeth-Jane. The reader now feels the keenest sympathy for her. She, too, suffers from an arbitrary fate that uncannily destroys one's happiness and security. However, the arrival of the pretty stranger at this point introduces a new note in the story and provides a momentary hope for Elizabeth-Jane. We are now so aware of Hardy's practice of involving every new character in the action that we look forward to the events precipitated by the introduction of Elizabeth-Jane's new friend.

The reader should notice the breadth of Hardy's knowl-edge of history, art, and folklore, as his allusions here reveal.

jowned   jolted. The expression would seem to mean, "Damn it, so am I", or "Be damned, so am I!"

Princess Ida   in Tennyson's poem, *The Princess*

wimbling   boring a hole, or piercing as with a wimble

the Constantines   Emperors of Rome, father and son. Constantine the Great moved the capital of the Roman Empire from Rome to Byzantium, whose name was changed to Constantinople. Constantine II ruled for a short time after his father's death.

Karnac   In Brittany: Carnac. Over two miles of parallel monoliths.

Austerlitz   in 1805, the battle in which Napoleon defeated the Russians and the Austrians

leery   tired

QUESTION

Does Elizabeth-Jane's decision to be the pretty stranger's companion indicate that her life will be comparatively happy from this point on?

CHAPTER 21

SYNOPSIS: ELIZABETH-JANE MOVES TO HIGH-PLACE HALL

Elizabeth-Jane, "almost with a lover's feeling," stealthily visits High-Place Hall, the chief town topic now that word is out of a new resident there. She is impressed by the easy but rather secret access the house has from many directions. Despite the fact that the appearance of the house suggests intrigue, she is anxious to move there immediately. Henchard also visits the house, but Elizabeth-Jane hides when she hears footsteps. Thus, neither of them is conscious of the other's identity.

After Henchard's return home, she realizes that his harshness has turned to "absolute indifference." She asks if she might leave his home to take employment which will advance her knowledge and manners. He readily agrees and is somewhat relieved that she is going. Elizabeth-Jane once again meets the stranger at the churchyard and learns her name is Miss Templeman. It is decided that Elizabeth-Jane will move into High-Place Hall that very evening, although Miss Templeman wonders if it might not be better to avoid mentioning High-Place Hall to Henchard. Henchard, upon learning of Elizabeth-Jane's immediate departure, tries at the last minute to persuade her to remain. Elizabeth-Jane tells him that she will not be far and that if he should need her she will return immediately. Henchard is surprised when he learns of her destination.

DISCUSSION

This chapter completes the work of the last two—that is, stripping Henchard of his remaining affectionate ties to others. The fact that Elizabeth-Jane cannot be dissuaded from leaving shows that she is acquiring an independent character. The reader assumes that the pretty stranger who takes such an interest in Elizabeth-Jane is Lucetta. This inference, coupled with the grotesque descriptions of High-Place Hall and Henchard's clandestine visit there, hints to the reader that new directions, possibly unpleasant, will be taken soon.

Hardy's professional interest in architecture is again evident in the description of High-Place Hall. His reasons for placing it so near the center of town rather than on the outskirts will become clear.

QUESTION

What parallels in his previous conduct can you name for Henchard's belated request for Elizabeth-Jane to stay?

CHAPTER 22

SYNOPSIS: LUCETTA WAITS FOR HENCHARD'S CALL

Henchard had gone to High-Place Hall the same evening as Elizabeth-Jane because he had received a letter from Lucetta informing him of her new residence. However, Henchard learns that a Miss Templeman is the only resident, not a Miss Le Sueur (the name by which Henchard had known Lucetta in Jersey). Henchard receives another note from Lucetta informing him that she has taken the name of Templeman—from a recently deceased aunt—in order to keep her real identity secret. Henchard also learns that Lucetta has received a large inheritance from the aunt, and he immediately feels that now would be a proper time to pursue his marriage plans. He is amused that Lucetta has invited Elizabeth-Jane to be her companion since this will give him a reason to visit High-Place Hall. Henchard immediately goes to see Lucetta, but is told she is engaged. This annoys him, and he decides to punish her by delaying his next visit.

A few days pass and Henchard has not yet visited Lucetta. Elizabeth-Jane and Lucetta have become quite friendly, though Elizabeth-Jane now surmises that she is the less flighty of the two. Lucetta discloses her Jersey background even though she had resolved not to do so. Lucetta feels that Henchard will not come since he does not want to see Elizabeth-Jane. She therefore sends Elizabeth-Jane on some errands, writes a note to Henchard inviting him to come immediately, and awaits his arrival. A visitor is finally shown into her drawing room, but to Lucetta's surprise the man is not Henchard.

DISCUSSION

Some interesting developments occur in this chapter. Hardy shows that the clever deception which Henchard had practiced in order to marry Susan is being repeated in variation by Lucetta. Furthermore, the reader begins to doubt Henchard's ability to hold any affectionate ties since the question of love does not enter much into his consideration of marriage to Lucetta. He seems to be thinking of it primarily as a commercial alliance, although his sentiments "gathered around Lucetta before they had grown dry."

Lucetta's room overlooking the market has already become an important vantage point and a center of interest.

mon ami étourderie   mon ami, my friend; *étourderie,* lack of concern — thoughtless action; thoughtlessness (French)

carrefour crossroads, open square (French)

gibbous rounded, seemingly hunch-backed

Titian famous Venetian artist

(1477–1576)

netting making netting, the groundwork for delicate embroidery

cyma-recta an architectural term: a curved profile partly concave and partly convex, the convex part nearest the wall (often referring to a curved molding)

QUESTION

Why does Lucetta emerge as an interesting character in spite of Hardy's partly stock account of her as the typically flighty Frenchwoman?

CHAPTER 23

SYNOPSIS: A MUTUAL ATTRACTION

The visitor is Donald Farfrae, "fair, fresh, and slenderly handsome," come to call upon Elizabeth-Jane after receiving permission to court her. At first Lucetta and Donald are embarrassed, but a mutual attraction takes hold, and they pass the time flirting with each other. Overhearing a business transaction from the window and upset by the conditions, Donald goes down to the market for a moment to hire a young man who had been faced with abandoning his sweetheart in order to retain a position. Lucetta is impressed by Donald's romantic and humane spirit. He leaves, but only after they decide that he should visit again: "Farfrae was shown out, it having entirely escaped him that he had called to see Elizabeth." About three minutes after Donald's departure Henchard arrives. Lucetta, infatuated with her new-found acquaintance, sends word that since she has a headache she won't detain him. Henchard leaves, and Lucetta resolves to keep Elizabeth-Jane with her as a "watchdog to keep her father off."

DISCUSSION

Lucetta and Donald become infatuated with each other. Of course Lucetta does not know of Elizabeth-Jane's feelings toward Donald. Even though Donald tells her that he has come to visit Elizabeth-Jane, Lucetta does not end the interview immediately but prolongs it into an emotional flirtation. Though she states emphatically that she is not a *coquette,* we learn by this behavior that she is. Lucetta several times mentions "love" and "lovers" in her conversation with Donald. She is also flighty and deceptive—witness her decision to keep Elizabeth-Jane to fend off Henchard immediately after packing her off so as to encourage Henchard. She is filled with fluctuating emotions: "Her emotions rose, fell, undulated, filled her with wild surmise at their suddenness." Yet it would be unfair to judge her critically since our chief point of reference is Elizabeth-Jane's rather quiet, innocent, melancholy character. With her refusal to admit Henchard, Lucetta appears to have ended all possibility of their marriage.

Hardy often adds pleasing strokes of humor, as when Lucetta invites Donald to sit down: "He hesitated, looked at the chair, thought there was no danger in it (though there was), and sat down." The passage quietly reminds us of Farfrae's cautious nature in sizing up what is probably a spindly "French" chair, and adds a pleasant touch of ambiguity with "though there was."

kerseymere fine wool woven so that diagonal lines appear on the material
St. Helier large town in Jersey
waggon-tilts the canvas coverings of wagons
Dan Cupid Roman god of love. "Dan" is applied humorously to mean "Sir"

QUESTION

How would you project the changes that will occur in the lives of the main characters as a result of Lucetta's and Donald's mutual attraction?

CHAPTER 24

SYNOPSIS: LUCETTA TELLS ELIZABETH-JANE A STORY

Lucetta and Elizabeth-Jane now pass the days of the week in anxious anticipation of Saturday's market when they might be able to catch a glimpse of Farfrae from their window. A new seeding machine called a horse-drill is brought to town and Lucetta—wearing her beautiful new dress "of a deep cherry color" from London—suggests that they go to see the machine. While examining the drill, they meet Michael Henchard, whom Elizabeth-Jane immediately introduces to Lucetta. Michael gruffly criticizes the machine's function and departs quickly. Before he leaves, Elizabeth-Jane overhears him state under his breath to Lucetta: "You refused to see me!" Elizabeth-Jane reflects upon the incident but appears not to realize that a relationship exists between Lucetta and Henchard.

They meet Donald as he examines the new machine. It was upon his recommendation that the modern piece of farm equipment has been purchased. He explains to the two ladies that the machine will revolutionize farming. It becomes obvious to

Elizabeth-Jane that Donald and Lucetta have grown fond of each other.

A few days later, desiring to get advice about her own rather difficult position, Lucetta reveals her past to Elizabeth-Jane, but tells the story as if it had happened to another woman. Her main question is what should the other "she" do now that "she" has grown fond of a second man. Elizabeth-Jane refuses to answer so delicate a question. However, she knows that Lucetta had been referring to herself.

DISCUSSION

The plot becomes more involved. Farfrae is advancing in Lucetta's favor while Henchard declines. Though Elizabeth-Jane does not know of a relationship between Lucetta and Henchard, she is saddened by the interest in each other that Donald and Lucetta already show. Not only has fate taken away most of Michael Henchard's happiness, but it also appears that chance and blind circumstance are plotting to do a similarly thorough job on Elizabeth-Jane's life. Yet we admire increasingly the uncomplaining girl and respect her silent stoicism.

The seed-drill accents the differences between Henchard and Farfrae. Henchard's stubborn conservatism evokes sympathy, but progress is clearly on Farfrae's side.

QUESTION

What can you discern in the episode of the horse-drill about Hardy's attitudes toward technological progress?

CHAPTER 25

SYNOPSIS: LUCETTA CHOOSES DONALD

Both Donald and Henchard call upon Lucetta. Lucetta insists that Elizabeth-Jane be present when Donald calls. During these visits Elizabeth-Jane sees only too plainly that Donald's old passion for her has disappeared and that he is now in love with Lucetta. At these times she remains in the room until she can conveniently excuse herself.

Michael, having grown more possessive of Lucetta now that she has become inaccessible, visits her and proposes marriage. Lucetta puts off the decision, and Michael half-realizes that he has been rejected. Though he may suspect a rival, he does not as yet know of Donald. Elizabeth-Jane accepts Donald's rejection of her since she considers Lucetta far more desirable. However, as the days pass she cannot really understand Henchard's complete unconcern for her welfare. After all, she has never to her knowledge caused him any grief. Out of long experience with "the wreck of each day's wishes," Elizabeth-Jane becomes reconciled to being rejected by the two men in her life who have come to symbolize her happiness.

DISCUSSION

Though much occurs in this chapter concerning Donald and Henchard, most of the events are seen as they affect Elizabeth-Jane and appear to her understanding. In this manner Hardy emphasizes his theme of blind fate when he talks of Elizabeth-Jane's stoicism: "She had learnt the lesson of renunciation . . ."

QUESTION

Are your sympathies with or against Lucetta's cry: "I won't be a slave to the past—I'll love where I choose"?

CHAPTER 26

SYNOPSIS: HENCHARD HIRES AND FIRES JOPP

Henchard's faint suspicion that his rival might be Donald abates when the latter shows his ignorance that the lady in Henchard's past is Lucetta. But not long after, Henchard divines the rivalry when he and Donald are having tea with Lucetta. Elizabeth-Jane, who is witness to the awkward threesome, watches them and begins to feel that they are all behaving like fools. With "vitalized antagonism" toward Donald, Henchard hires Jopp, the man who had originally applied for the position

of manager, and instructs him to try every honest way of forcing Farfrae out of business. Jopp is only too willing since he
nurses a bitter grudge against Farfrae as the man who replaced
him. Henchard, unaware that "characters deteriorate in time of
need," quiets Elizabeth-Jane's distrust of Jopp "with a sharp
rebuff."

Henchard consults a local weather diviner named Mr.
Fall. He pays him for reading the future and predicting a very
wet harvest season. As a result of this less-than-reliable information, Henchard speculates heavily upon rainy harvest weather.
However, the weather changes and the harvest promises to be
a glorious one. Prices go down and Henchard has to sell his
speculative purchases at a great loss in order to meet current
obligations. He is forced to mortgage much of his property and
corn-holdings to the bank. Furious at Jopp for not advising
against the speculation, Henchard dismisses him. Jopp bitterly
vows vengeance against Henchard.

DISCUSSION

As the rivalry between Henchard and Donald grows more
keen, Hardy plants another seed of possible destruction. Jopp
is aware that Lucetta comes from Jersey and that Henchard had
often done business there. Fate and chance now will bear heavily
upon every continuing chapter. Hardy describes how directly
the well-being of the farmers depends upon fluctuations of the
weather. The great difference between Henchard and Farfrae
is thrown into bold relief when Henchard visits the soothsayer
for a prediction. It becomes clear that Henchard lives in the
past and Donald is the man of the future. Henchard's visit to
Mr. Fall recalls the statement in Chapter 2 that "there was
something fetichistic in this man's beliefs."

pis aller   the last resource
  (French)
Alastor   a deity of revenge
water-tights   boots
bell-board   a table or board on
  which were placed small bells
  that were rung at the appropriate time by a number of
  ringers. (Thus, the tune depended on each ringer; hence,
  Casterbridge depended on the

surrounding villages and ham-
  lets for its commerce.)
the evil   scrofula. A toad-bag
  contained the legs of frogs, and
  was worn around the neck. This
  superstition held that the toad-
  bag was a cure for scrofula
  (sometimes called "the king's
  evil").
dungmixen   dung-heap, dunghill

QUESTION

Why does Hardy have Henchard visit Mr. Fall rather than simply guessing wrong about the weather himself?

CHAPTER 27

SYNOPSIS: HENCHARD FORCES LUCETTA TO CONSENT

Farfrae begins buying grain now that promise of a fair harvest has driven prices down. The weather quickly turns damp, and it is clear that Farfrae has once again been shrewd.

An accident occurs beneath Lucetta's window, involving Henchard's and Donald's hay wagons. Lucetta and Elizabeth-Jane both side with Donald's driver. Henchard is brought to the scene where he gives instructions to Constable Stubberd. The constable tells him that there is only one case pending in the town court, that of a disorderly old woman. Henchard tells him that he will hear the case in the absence from town of Mayor Chalkfield.

After setting things right for the moment, Henchard attempts to call on Lucetta, who has returned home. She sends word that she has "an engagement to go out."

Henchard decides to wait in the shadows in order to learn if Donald might be her caller. Donald arrives at nine o'clock, and together he and Lucetta walk to the fields where the townsmen are reaping by moonlight. Henchard decides to follow them. The couple take a twisting route and soon double back upon Henchard who is forced to hide. From hiding he hears them declare their love for each other. He leaves and returns to Lucetta's home. Without knocking he enters the house and waits for her. Upon her return he threatens to reveal the past if she refuses to marry him. With Elizabeth-Jane as a witness, Lucetta agrees to the marriage. Lucetta faints, and Elizabeth-Jane upbraids Henchard for forcing her, for Lucetta "cannot bear much." Henchard leaves, and Elizabeth-Jane remains baffled by the strong hold he has over Lucetta.

DISCUSSION

Donald's business prosperity rankles morbidly in Henchard's mind. Hardy again emphasizes Henchard's "fetichism" by showing him wondering if someone has placed a curse on him. Henchard even believes that Donald will soon become mayor. We see that Henchard's brutal threat of blackmail against Lucetta is not a result of his desire to marry her, but of an unholy wish to beat Farfrae, to hurt him, to take something away from him. As usual, there is no love motivating Henchard's behavior.

zwailing swaying, shifting

gawk-hammer way awkward, ridiculous

"you would have zeed me!" you would have *seen* me

thill horse the horse which is harnessed between the shafts of the wagon

dand the word "dandy" is left uncompleted

giddying in a rotating or whirling fashion

no'thern a dialect word; wandering in mind, or incoherent

QUESTION

Is Henchard's insistence that Lucetta marry him motivated partly, entirely, or not at all by the question of honor in keeping a promise?

CHAPTER 28

SYNOPSIS: THE JUDGE IS JUDGED

Henchard, being a magistrate, is required to preside in the case of the old woman accused of creating an obscene nuisance.

In court Henchard fails to recognize the old crone, although she looks faintly familiar. However, after the arresting officer gives his story, the old woman tells the court that twenty years ago she witnessed the sale of a wife. She then points to Henchard and declares that he is the man who sold his wife. She concludes by saying that he has no right to sit in judgment over her. Henchard recognizes the furmity woman and is shocked. However, he agrees with her, corroborates the story, and leaves his place of judgment.

Her servant tells Lucetta of the furmity woman's story. Lucetta, who had always believed that Henchard's wife had been presumed dead, is taken aback. She decides that she must leave Casterbridge and vacation for a few days at Port-Bredy. Henchard calls upon her a number of times only to learn that she has left town. When he calls a few days later he learns that she has returned, but has gone for a walk on the turnpike road toward Port-Bredy.

DISCUSSION

Henchard's past has finally caught up with him. The turn of events is somewhat unexpected. Even more unexpected is Henchard's complete corroboration of the furmity woman's story. Despite all his shortcomings, Henchard must be respected for a rough kind of moral virtue. It would have been easy for him to deny the furmity woman's story, since she wasn't believed in the first place. However, the ironic justice becomes plain to him, and since we have become acquainted with his quick starts and sudden decisions, his confession is not unnatural.

Shallow and Silence in Shakespeare's *King Henry IV*, Part II. They are comic characters and serve as country justices of the peace.

ashlar a roughhewn square block of stone

Hannah Dominy from Latin *Anno Domine* (A.D., in the year of our Lord). A slight bit of satirizing of the rather ignorant type of justice of the peace. The word "instinct" which precedes the corruption of the legal phrase should be "instance."

wambling weaving, wobbling

turmit-hit turnip-head, turnip-top, idiot

"you son of a bee," "dee me if I haint" the constable does not want to swear in court.

larry commotion or disturbance

QUESTION

What are some of the reasons the author has the furmity woman unmask Henchard while he is sitting as judge rather than in the street or at home?

CHAPTER 29

SYNOPSIS: LUCETTA'S REVELATION

Lucetta is a mile out of town on the road to Port-Bredy waiting for Donald. Elizabeth-Jane comes to meet her when suddenly they are confronted by a ferocious bull. The enraged animal pursues them into a barn where they are forced to flee from his maddened charging. Henchard arrives, subdues the bull, and rescues them. He takes the hysterical Lucetta home.

Elizabeth-Jane, who had returned to the barn to retrieve Lucetta's muff, encounters Donald Farfrae in his carriage. She explains the events. Donald appears very upset by the news, but decides that he had better not seek out Lucetta for fear of intruding upon the two. He drops Elizabeth-Jane off and returns to his house, where his things are being packed for a move.

Henchard, meanwhile, has accompanied Lucetta to town. He informs her that he is willing to release her from an immediate marriage. She states that she would like to repay him with a large amount of cash in the same manner as he had been of financial assistance to her in the past. He refuses to take money, but asks her instead to say they will soon be married to a Mr. Grower, one of his heaviest creditors. Grower will then not press Henchard for immediate cash. He will then have sufficient time to raise the money. Lucetta cannot do this. She explains that when she learned that Henchard had sold his first wife, she feared to put her safety in his hands. She tells him that she and Donald Farfrae were married this week in Port-Bredy, and that Mr. Grower had been a witness to it.

Henchard is infuriated since he feels that she has broken her word. Lucetta tells him that her promise had been made under compulsion and before she had heard how he sold his first wife. She begs him not to tell Donald of the past. Henchard rages at her and once again threatens to tell the world of their past intimacy.

DISCUSSION

The chance appearance of the furmity woman has resulted in Lucetta's marriage to Farfrae. We are aware of Henchard's hold over Lucetta, and we are sure that he will take advantage of it in his rage. This chapter reveals Hardy's minute, but architectural structuring of the novel. All things fall into place, though the reader may feel somewhat pressed by the chance occurrence of so many events. Though the furmity woman may have come to Casterbridge by chance, it must be remembered that if Henchard had not committed an enormity years ago, the chance arrival of the furmity woman would not have mattered in the least. Thus we see that a man is never free of his past; he can set his own fate in motion and afterward have not the slightest control over it.

Yahoo in *Gulliver's Travels,* by Swift. An animal that looks like man, but behaves like a dumb, vicious beast

the Thames Tunnel completed in 1843. Hardy might be referring to toys that represented the tunnel. He might also be referring to the stereoscope, a viewing device that represented pictures in seemingly three-di-

mensional perspective.

Gurth's collar a swineherd in Scott's *Ivanhoe* who wore a brass ring around his neck, which could only be filed through to free him of the collar.

a pensioner of Farfrae's wife to be put on relief by Farfrae's wife, or to be financially dependent on Farfrae's wife

QUESTION

Do you think Henchard will stand by his threat to reveal his former relations with Lucetta?

CHAPTER 30

SYNOPSIS: ELIZABETH-JANE LEAVES HIGH-PLACE HALL

Donald arranges to have his belongings moved to Lucetta's home. When he arrives Lucetta informs him that she would like Elizabeth-Jane to remain and Donald consents. Elizabeth-Jane tells Lucetta that she fully understands the implications of the story she had been told of another woman's past, and that her father figures in Lucetta's life. She feels strongly that Lucetta should, out of propriety, marry Henchard. Lucetta says that her promise to Henchard was made under constraint. She reveals her marriage to Donald. Even though Elizabeth-Jane has decided immediately that she must leave the house because of her feelings toward Donald, she tells Lucetta that she will decide upon the issue later.

That night Elizabeth-Jane removes her belongings to a residence across the street from Henchard. She leaves a note explaining her move for Lucetta and returns to her new room

to consider her prospects. The villagers have by now heard of
the marriage and are busy conjecturing whether Donald will
stay in business or live off his wife.

DISCUSSION

Elizabeth-Jane is a stickler for propriety, is, "indeed, almost
vicious" in her condemnation of any form of waywardness. It
is not hard to understand this, since the confusing events of
her past life might appear to her to be the results of a neglect
of the legal and social mores. Hardy, however, is guilty of
forced logic in showing her disapproval of Lucetta's choosing
Farfrae over Henchard. His rather weak account of Elizabeth-
Jane as a homebody who never listens to gossip cannot make
convincing her ignorance of the furmity woman's revelation
and Henchard's corroboration.

"John Gilpin" a ballad by Wil-
liam Cowper (1731–1800)
Nathan tones the prophet Nathan was damning in his on-
slaught against King David's
marriage to Bath-Sheba

Ovid famous Latin poet (43
B.C.–18 A.D.). The line is from
his *Metamorphoses:* "Though I
approve of the better things I
see, I follow after the worse."

QUESTION

Compared with the other characters, how would you view
Elizabeth-Jane's character and personality as they might lead to
a happy and satisfying life?

CHAPTER 31

SYNOPSIS: HENCHARD'S BANKRUPTCY

After the furmity woman's revelation, Henchard's fortunes and esteem diminish rapidly. One of his heavy debtors
fails and bad judgment by one of his employees causes a serious
financial loss. Bankruptcy proceedings are instituted against
Henchard in which his creditors take possession of all his property. He is at his lowest point: "The black hair and whiskers
were the same as ever, but a film of ash was over the rest." At
the proceedings, Henchard offers his remaining property, the

loose change in his money-bag, and his gold watch. The creditors refuse to take these last remaining possessions, but instead praise him for his extraordinary honesty in giving over all his worldly goods. Much affected, Henchard leaves, sells his watch for the first offer, and brings the cash to one of his minor creditors.

Henchard moves to Jopp's cottage by Priory Mill. Elizabeth-Jane, moved to compassion by his terrible downfall, attempts to see him. However, Henchard is at home to no one, including Elizabeth-Jane. After an unsuccessful attempt to see her stepfather, Elizabeth-Jane passes by Henchard's former place of business. She learns that Donald Farfrae has bought the property and taken over all of Henchard's employees. Though the salary is slightly lower, the men are happy with Farfrae's working conditions. Furthermore, whereas Henchard's business had been conducted by rule-of-thumb procedures, Donald has instituted sound business techniques and modern innovations.

DISCUSSION

Henchard's rapid decline in fortune and prestige is as complete as Donald Farfrae's rise. Elizabeth-Jane is more alone now than she has ever been. All the elements have conspired to reverse the positions of the characters, and Farfrae has won out completely, even in love.

An odd note is sounded by the curious alliance that Henchard maintains with Jopp. There is certainly no friendship between the two men, since Henchard blamed Jopp for allowing him to speculate on the weather, and Jopp despises Henchard for dismissing him. The one connective would be their mutual hatred for Donald Farfrae. One gets the feeling that Jopp has taken in Henchard for the purpose of taunting him with his failure, and that Henchard is using Jopp as a scourge. Given Henchard's compulsion to do the self-destructive thing, there is an ironic justice in his identification with the village's most conspicuous failure.

One of the creditors is a "reserved young man named Boldwood." Boldwood is an important character in Hardy's much earlier novel, *Far from the Madding Crowd*.

QUESTION

What elements of Henchard's character come to the fore in the bankruptcy episodes?

CHAPTER 32

SYNOPSIS: FARFRAE HIRES
HENCHARD

Henchard begins to haunt one of the town's bridges which has become known for its attraction to failures and suicides. One afternoon Jopp encounters him on the bridge and states that Donald and Lucetta have purchased Henchard's old house and are moving in. He also tells him that the man who bought Henchard's best furniture at the auction was in reality bidding for Donald Farfrae. Jopp departs well satisfied that he has wounded Henchard. Henchard's bitterness is increased at the vagaries of fortune. Donald Farfrae arrives in a gig to see Henchard. He repeats the rumor that Henchard is planning to emigrate and asks him to remain in Casterbridge, just as Henchard had once asked him to stay. Donald generously offers Henchard lodging within the same house that he and Lucetta have just purchased. Henchard visualizes this arrangement with repugnance and refuses outright. Donald then offers to give back to Henchard all the furniture which might hold sentimental value for him. For a moment Henchard is struck by Donald's magnanimity and says, "I—sometimes think I've wronged 'ee!"

Later Elizabeth-Jane hears that Henchard is confined to his room with a cold. She immediately goes to him and, after a preliminary refusal by Henchard, administers to him and sets his room in comfortable order. Due to Elizabeth-Jane's repeated visits and tender care, Henchard regains his strength and a more cheerful outlook. Judging that hard work never hurt a young man—Henchard is not much over forty—he applies to Farfrae as a day-laborer. Farfrae employs him, but is careful to relay instructions and orders through a third person. And thus Henchard who once worked as a hay-trusser dressed in clean, bright clothes appears in the yards he used to own; now he wears "the remains of an old blue cloth suit of his gentlemanly times, a rusty silk hat, and a once black satin stock, soiled and shabby."

The days go by and Henchard watches Donald and Lucetta. His old jealousy and hatred return, especially when he hears that Farfrae may be chosen mayor in a few years.

One day Elizabeth-Jane hears a villager say that "Michael Henchard have busted out drinking" again. The twenty-one year "gospel oath" has come to an end. Elizabeth-Jane immediately sets out to find him.

DISCUSSION

Whereas in the last chapter all of Henchard's property had been auctioned off and Donald had purchased Henchard's former place of business, this chapter is necessary to complete the reversal of fortune. Donald purchases Henchard's house and furniture. Only one more point need be added to furnish the final irony. Henchard himself answers fate's call and takes employment as a day-laborer in Donald's business. It would appear now that Henchard can go no lower; with the hint of Donald's likelihood of becoming mayor, it seems that he can go no higher. The close proximity of Henchard to the newly married couple is what begins to work upon his mind. It is evident that it lies within Henchard's character to wreak some kind of new havoc now that he has begun to drink again.

QUESTION

What other conditions besides his drinking now repeat Henchard's position when we first met him twenty years earlier?

CHAPTER 33

SYNOPSIS: HENCHARD'S RESENTMENT IS INFLAMED

One Sunday Henchard takes part in the after-church discussion and song-fest which the townspeople and the choir members hold at the Three Mariners. He sees Donald and Lucetta leaving church, and under the influence of drink, forces the members of the choir to sing one of the *Psalms,* which contains a curse against the man of "ill-got riches." When Farfrae passes, Henchard tells the dismayed company that the curse was meant for him. Elizabeth-Jane arrives and takes Henchard home. While walking with him she hears Henchard make veiled threats against Donald. She resolves to warn Donald as soon as it becomes necessary.

Henchard's misery is intensified by the pitying looks he gets from Abel Whittle. Elizabeth-Jane offers to help Henchard in Abel's place. Her reason for helping is to observe Henchard and Donald when they come face to face. One day Lucetta accompanies Donald into the yard, but wanders away and accidentally confronts Henchard. Henchard bitterly feigns servility to Lucetta. The next morning Henchard receives a note from Lucetta which asks him to behave with less bitterness toward her if they should meet again. Henchard realizes that this letter places Lucetta in a compromising position, but he destroys it rather than use it against her.

Elizabeth-Jane begins to bring Henchard tea in order to keep him away from stronger drink. One day she arrives to find Henchard and Donald standing near the open door on the top floor of the corn building. Elizabeth-Jane sees Henchard make a furtive gesture as if he intended to push Donald out the opening to his death. This so frightens her that she resolves to inform Donald of her stepfather's mental state.

DISCUSSION

This chapter shows Henchard becoming more and more bold in his threats against Farfrae as a result of his heavy drinking. As time passes, Donald begins to look upon Henchard as an ordinary worker. Of course this is a hint that such an attitude will have its effect upon Henchard. The one implausible element in the chapter is Lucetta's ignorance of Henchard's employment. Even though Donald has taken pains to ignore the new relationship between Henchard and himself, in a town which seems to thrive upon gossip it would appear strange that such a newsworthy item as Henchard's ironic employment had not reached Lucetta's ears. Even stranger is the fact that Donald has not informed her.

The loft is a vivid and appropriate setting for the incident Elizabeth-Jane spies when bringing tea.

Stonehenge a famous monument dating back to prehistoric times, consisting of stone pillars placed in a circular fashion

"We've let back our strings. . . ." We've loosened the strings (on the instruments).

rantipole rubbish rough or boisterous language or verses sung to accompany a procession which contains an acted out scene of a man beating his wife (the *rantipole ride*)

trap a trap-door

QUESTION

What can be said to justify Henchard's bitter sarcasm when he encounters Lucetta?

CHAPTER 34

SYNOPSIS: HENCHARD READS TO FARFRAE

Elizabeth-Jane meets Farfrae early one morning and warns him that Henchard may try "to do something—that would injure you." Donald makes light of the warning, but later receives a similar warning from the town clerk. We learn that Donald had offered the first fifty pounds if the town council would underwrite the remainder of the costs to install Henchard in a seed shop. Because of the disconcerting information Donald has to review the plans, and he cancels the negotiations with the owner of the seed shop. The disappointed owner tells Henchard that the council had planned to give him a new start but that Donald had ruined it.

Donald confides to Lucetta that he is upset because of Henchard's enmity. She suggests that they sell out and move away. Donald gives the thought consideration. At that moment Alderman Vatt arrives with the news that Mayor Chalkfield has died. He tells Donald that the Council would like to elect him mayor. Because it is the town's wish, Donald says he will accept the office if it is bestowed upon him. It seems that now, despite Lucetta's fears and his own worry over Henchard, he must stay because destiny requires it.

Lucetta meets Henchard by accident in the market-place. "Imprudence incarnate," she asks him once again to return her old letters. Henchard says he does not have them, but that he will consider her request. Next evening the town bell announces a new mayor. Henchard has remembered that the letters are among papers in the safe of his former house and arranges with Donald to come and retrieve them. Fortified with drink, Henchard arrives at Mayor Farfrae's home quite late. He gets the letters and morbidly reads their contents to Farfrae. This grotesque conduct seems to give Henchard pleasure, since at this point he holds the future happiness of Lucetta and Donald in his hand. However, he cannot bring himself to reveal to Donald that Lucetta had written the letters: "His quality was such that he could have annihilated them both in the heat of action; but to accomplish the deed by oral poison was beyond the nerve of his enmity."

DISCUSSION

Henchard's bitterness now takes concrete form. The misunderstanding of the seed shop incident inflames him, and Farfrae's election as Mayor adds still more to his enmity. When Lucetta imprudently asks Henchard for the letters, she unwittingly opens another means whereby Henchard can indulge his own self-pity and still flirt somewhat sadistically with the idea of revealing to Donald both the contents of the letters and the name of their author.

With his election as Mayor of Casterbridge, Farfrae now owns everything Henchard had owned when they met.

QUESTION

What would Farfrae's reaction be if he learned of the relationship between Henchard and Lucetta in the past?

CHAPTER 35

SYNOPSIS: HENCHARD AND LUCETTA AT THE RING

In a flashback we learn that Lucetta has overheard Michael reading the letters to her husband. She fears he has revealed all, but when Farfrae retires that night she learns "to her joyous amazement" that he knows nothing of her past. The next morning she writes to Henchard and asks to meet him at the Ring. She decides to present herself humbly and to beg for the return of her letters.

At sunset she meets Henchard at the Ring. The surroundings are gloomy, as usual, but the area brings to Henchard's mind his meeting with Susan, another woman whom he had wronged. This realization causes his heart to melt, and when he sees Lucetta so plainly dressed and so miserable, he relents. He feels that she has stupidly placed herself in a very compromising position by meeting him. He therefore loses all interest in her and promises that her letters will be returned the next morning.

DISCUSSION

Lucetta is shown to be losing her youthful beauty. Apparently the strain and suspense which Henchard has caused have begun to take their toll. By having Henchard promise to return the letters, Hardy is absolving him of any further intentions of destroying the marriage. However, the letters seem far too important to be dropped so suddenly.

Henchard appears in a generous light when he takes pity on Lucetta. His feeling that she is "very small deer to hunt" reveals that largeness of outlook that contributes so much to his stature as tragic hero.

QUESTION

What story developments do you expect from Henchard's promise to return Lucetta's letters?

CHAPTER 36

SYNOPSIS: JOPP OPENS THE LETTERS

Lucetta returns home to find Jopp waiting for her. He asks her to put in a few good words with Donald about employing him. She replies that she knows nothing about him, and that it is not her custom to interfere in her husband's business. Lucetta ends the interview abruptly for fear that Donald will miss her.

Jopp returns to his cottage, and Henchard asks him to deliver a parcel to Mrs. Farfrae. Jopp states that he will do it. After Henchard retires, Jopp begins to think about the connection between Henchard and Lucetta. Because Jopp had come from Jersey, he knows that Henchard had once courted her. His bitterness at Lucetta for refusing to speak to Farfrae intensifies his curiosity, so Jopp opens the package and finds the letters.

While on his way to deliver the package, Jopp encounters Mother Cuxsom and Nance Mockridge, who invite him to an inn called Peter's Finger in Mixen Lane, a place of evil repute near Casterbridge. At the gathering, when the furmity woman asks Jopp what the parcel contains, his bitterness at Lucetta comes out and he reveals the contents. Jopp proceeds to read the letters to the assembled company. Soon afterward a stranger appears on his way to Casterbridge. He hears the rogues in the tavern discussing a "skimmity-ride," and learns that it is a lower-class form of making fun of a married couple when the wife has not been altogether faithful. Since the stranger will be residing in Casterbridge for a while, and desiring some kind of entertainment, he gives the assembly of thieves and poachers a gold sovereign to cover the initial cost of the old custom. The townspeople begin to plan the skimmity-ride.

The next morning Jopp delivers the parcel to Lucetta, who burns the letters immediately.

DISCUSSION

The "Peter's Finger" episode is unusual in that the villagers become participants in the action rather than commentators merely. Hence the emphasis on them is not just the addition of local color or explanation but is an important new plot development as well.

dogs   the iron bars on which the logs are placed in a fireplace

Adulam   haven for people with troubles and difficulties

lifeholders, copy-holders   lifeholders held a lifetime lease to their homes and land. Copyholders did not own original legal deeds.

Ashton . . . Ravenswood   characters in Scott's *Bride of Lammermoor*. Ashton sees Ravenswood disappear (having sunk into quicksand).

swingels   part of a flail

oven-pyle   chips of wood for lighting a fire

skimmity-ride   skimmington-ride: a rowdy procession which is intended to make fun of a man whose wife is shrewish or unfaithful.

get it in train   to get it started

QUESTION

What is the significance of the appearance of the stranger in Mixen Lane?

CHAPTER 37

SYNOPSIS: HENCHARD GREETS THE ROYAL VISITOR

The town receives word that a royal personage will pass through Casterbridge in the near future. Mayor Farfrae and the council arrange for an elaborate reception. Henchard comes to the council meeting and asks to participate in the reception. Donald, with the concurrence of the council, refuses, whereupon Henchard makes plans to welcome the royal visitor by himself.

The royal visitor is escorted into the packed, spruced-up town by Donald and the members of the council. Lucetta indignantly tells some ladies looking on that Henchard had little or nothing to do with Donald's success. By this time, she doesn't like to be reminded that Henchard exists. Suddenly Henchard steps into the space before the Town Hall, waving a Union Jack (the British flag) and stretches out his arm to welcome the esteemed guest. Because it is Farfrae's duty as mayor to maintain decorum and safety for the visitor, he grabs Henchard by the collar and shoves him roughly into the crowd. The spectators, especially Lucetta and Elizabeth-Jane, are shocked by Henchard's low behavior. The royal personage, however, pretends "not to have noticed anything unusual."

The reader learns that the skimmity-ride will take place that night. Jopp confirms the plans and is now acting as a prime mover in the attempt to humiliate the Mayor. But two of the townspeople decide to write to the concerned parties and warn them of the impending demonstration.

DISCUSSION

It appears that Henchard, despite all common sense, still refuses to remain in his place. His character is as mercurial as it ever was, and the request he makes to the town council comes from a deep sense of the loss of his position, esteem, and wealth. He has always been subject to fits of rancor and bitterness, but with the resumption of his drinking these spells become more intense. Henchard's intrusion comes as a surprise to the reader, but Donald's rough treatment of him is con-

sidered justified by everyone in the crowd. The reader knows
that the public insult will only feed Henchard's fierce bitterness.

fête carillonnée   a celebration
complete with the pealing of
bells (French)

Royal unicorn   part of the Royal
emblem, or coat-of-arms of
Great Britain.

Calpurnia's cheek was pale   in
Shakespeare's *Julius Caesar*,
Brutus remarks that the cheek
of Caesar's wife—Calpurnia—
is pale. The reference is that

Farfrae (equivalent to a Caesar
among the crowd) has his
Brutus.

go snacks wi'en   go snacks with
him; to eat at his table; to live
with him

hontish   high-handed, haughty

to see that lady toppered   to see
that lady brought low—brought
to shame

QUESTION

What will be the effect on Lucetta of a skimmity-ride
involving her and Henchard at this point in her fortunes?

CHAPTER 38

SYNOPSIS: A DEADLY WRESTLING MATCH

Henchard, as maddened by Lucetta's scorn as Farfrae's
humiliating shove, resolves to wrestle Donald to the death. He
leaves a message for Donald to meet him in the corn storage
building and immediately goes there himself. Henchard knows
he is stronger than Donald, so he ties his left arm to his body,
rendering it useless in combat. Donald arrives later and Henchard calls him up to the loft. Michael faces him squarely and
says that Donald has snubbed him at work and disgraced him
in public. Now it is time to finish the wrestling match which
was begun that afternoon in front of the townspeople: " 'You
may be the one to cool first,' said Henchard grimly. 'Now this
is the case. Here be we, in this four-square loft, to finish out
that little wrestle you began this morning. There's the door,
forty foot above ground. One of us two puts the other out by
that door—the master stays inside. If he likes he may go down
afterwards and give the alarm that the other has fallen out by
accident—or he may tell the truth—that's his business. As the
strongest man I've tied one arm to take no advantage of 'ee.
D'ye understand? Then here's at 'ee.' "

Donald is no match against Henchard's strength, and soon he is half-out the open doorway with Henchard ready to hurl him to his death. But Henchard cannot commit the ultimate act of violence. He frees Donald and lies in a corner. The "womanliness" of his posture "sat tragically on the figure of so stern a piece of virility." Donald departs, and Henchard overhears Donald tell Whittle that he has been unexpectedly summoned to Weatherbury, thus causing him to cancel his intended plans of *traveling toward Budmouth.* Henchard is overcome by remorse and the desire to see Donald and seek his pardon. But Donald is out of town, and Henchard returns to his customary place on the bridge. From there he hears jumbled noises and rhythmical confusion coming from the town. So great is his consternation, he is not even curious about the unexplained noise.

DISCUSSION

Elizabeth-Jane's fears have become a reality. Michael Henchard has attempted to kill Donald Farfrae. But he is not a murderer, and it is his affection for the younger man that prevents him from snuffing out Donald's life. His physical superiority has not amounted to a victory, but a lowering of his opinion of himself.

It should be noted that only Whittle and Henchard know of Donald's change of destination when he leaves town.

Weltlust enjoyment or love of worldly pleasure (German)
"And here's a hand . . . thine" from Robert Burns's well-known song, "Auld Lang Syne." "Fiere" means friend or companion, and

"gie's" is a dialect contraction for "give us."
forward stripling upstart youngster
to close with Henchard to engage Henchard in combat

QUESTION

What do you expect Farfrae's future attitude toward Henchard to be?

CHAPTER 39

SYNOPSIS: THE SKIMMITY-RIDE

Though Donald's men have sent him a note asking him to go to Weatherbury as a pretext to spare him the sight of the skimmity-ride, they have taken no protective measures for Lucetta, since they believe she had carried on an illicit affair with Henchard. That evening the skimmity-ride is conveyed in a wild procession past Lucetta's house just as she is feeling most secure.

Elizabeth-Jane, aware of the vulgar display, rushes to Lucetta's house and begs her not to look. Lucetta, however, has heard two maids gossiping outside and cannot be restrained from observing the shame the townspeople wish to cast upon her. She goes to the window. There she gazes on the procession of the ignorant revellers accompanying a donkey upon whose back are the effigies of Henchard and herself tied together back to back by the elbows. The implication that the vulgar display reveals is only too clear to Lucetta. Driven to distraction by the fear her husband will see it and grow to hate her, she falls into an epileptic fit. The doctor is summoned, and since Lucetta is pregnant he fears her condition is highly critical. A man is immediately dispatched to bring Donald home from his supposed journey along the Budmouth Road. He has gone off to Weatherbury instead.

The feeble town constables are urged on by Mr. Grower, the witness at the Farfraes' wedding, to apprehend the perpetrators of the unlawful procession, but they are unable to discover who has taken part. They meet Jopp, but he claims to have seen nothing, and they finally go to the infamous Peter's Finger Inn in Mixen Lane, but there they discover only a quiet gathering. The reader knows that the members of the group at the inn had taken part in the skimmity-ride, but since they give false witness and establish alibis for each other, the constables are powerless to apprehend them.

DISCUSSION

The skimmington-ride has done more evil than its perpetrators had intended. Despite the good-hearted Elizabeth-Jane's efforts to hide the display from Lucetta, Lucetta sees the procession. It is strange that Hardy attributes the seizure to epilepsy. Though epilepsy may occur at unpredictable times, the disease is such that the sufferer usually has a history of seizures. Yet no mention has been made of such a history of sickness in Lucetta's past.

it mid be it might be
cleavers . . . rams'-horns Old
musical instruments or noise-
makers; a "croud" would be a
fiddle and "humstrums" would

be cranked instruments similar
to a hurdy-gurdy
Comus a masque by Milton
was with child an old form of
saying "was pregnant"

QUESTION

How would you judge Jopp's part in the cruel skimmity-ride by comparison with Henchard's misdeeds?

CHAPTER 40

SYNOPSIS: THE DEATH OF LUCETTA

Henchard is unable to sleep due to his consternation at having fought with Donald. He makes his way into Casterbridge and there sees the skimmington-ride. He immediately understands its meaning and the possible consequences. He goes directly to Donald's house, learns of Lucetta's illness, and tries to inform the inhabitants of Donald's true whereabouts. However, because of his recent unspeakable behavior, no one will believe him. He therefore sets out at a fast run to intercept Donald, knowing Lucetta's life could depend on her husband's presence.

He finally meets Donald at a lonely road-crossing. But, when Henchard tells Donald of his wife's sickness, Donald refuses to believe him. He feels that Henchard may have set a trap for him in order to finish what he had not done previously. "The very agitation and abruptness of Henchard" make Farfrae even more suspicious. He leaves toward his destination with Michael Henchard running after the gig, begging him to return.

Henchard returns and despairingly curses himself "like a less scrupulous Job." Throughout the night he makes inquiries about Lucetta's condition. Donald returns and that night stays beside his wife. During Donald's vigil, Lucetta informs him of her past relationship with Henchard. The extent of the information she imparts to Donald remains "Farfrae's secret alone."

Henchard has gone to his lodgings and there thinks of Elizabeth-Jane as his only comfort: "she seemed to him as a pinpoint of light." Jopp informs him that "a kind of traveller, or sea-captain of some sort" had called on Henchard. Henchard dismisses the information and that night, unable to sleep, paces to and fro before Donald's house. At dawn Michael learns that Lucetta has died.

DISCUSSION

This chapter is indeed a sad one. Hardy is bitterly denouncing man's evil treatment of his brother. One sentence in particular reinforces this judgment: "He went across, the sparrows in his way scarcely flying up from the road-litter, so little did they believe in human aggression at so early a time."

The introduction of a sea-captain creates a new pause for thought. Since Hardy seldom introduces a character unless there is an organic part for him to play in the unfolding plot, the reader assumes that the sea-captain will have some effect on the future action.

a less scrupulous Job   the biblical character Job, who only lived to do right, cursed the day of his birth when he was punished by God for no apparent reason. Hence, Henchard, not quite as conscientious in his desire to do good, also curses himself as Job did.

well-be-doing   a man who is well off, doing well

Lucifer   the planet Venus when it appears as the morning star

QUESTION

Who do you think the sea-captain is?

CHAPTER 41

SYNOPSIS: HENCHARD LIES TO THE CAPTAIN

Elizabeth-Jane visits Henchard on the morning of Lucetta's death. There Henchard, moved to genuine love for his stepdaughter, offers to prepare breakfast while she refreshes herself with sleep. He waits for her "as if it were an honor to have her in his house." While Elizabeth-Jane sleeps, Captain Newson, the sailor who had figured so prominently in Henchard's life, arrives. When he identifies himself, "Henchard's face and eyes seemed to die." Newson informs Henchard that, in order to be kind to Susan who had found their relationship untenable, he had arranged the story of his loss at sea. He is now wealthy, and has returned to claim his daughter. Impulsively, fearing that Elizabeth-Jane will leave him, Henchard tells Newson that Elizabeth-Jane had died more than a year before. Newson is terribly dejected and, taking Henchard's word at face value, leaves Casterbridge immediately. Elizabeth-Jane awakens but Henchard is afraid to ask her to stay for he is sure Newson will return and claim Elizabeth-Jane himself. He goes to Ten Hatches—the name of the junction where the river runs deep —and contemplates suicide. Suddenly he sees his exact image floating in the water. He has a superstitous change of heart and returns home to find Elizabeth-Jane awaiting him. He takes her to Ten Hatches where she discovers that the image he has seen is the effigy used in the skimmington-ride, thrown into the river by the revellers in order to destroy the evidence. Elizabeth-Jane quickly guesses Henchard's plans and asks to be allowed to live with him and take care of his needs. Henchard readily assents, and from that moment on becomes a new man. In his new cheerfulness he says that "it seems that even I be in Somebody's hand!"

DISCUSSION

The sea-captain who had looked for Henchard in the last chapter turns out to be Newson. Henchard is barely able to find a grain of happiness before it is threatened and wrenched from him. He is still impetuous, and the information he gives Newson of Elizabeth-Jane's death can only result in his utter estrangement from her if she should learn of it. He knows this, yet his reason for lying is prompted by love, an emotion which is, to say the least, alien to Henchard's temperament. The effect of Elizabeth-Jane's concern and care is like a medication upon Henchard. He finds a momentary belief in a Supreme Power, changes in outlook, and is, for the moment, rejuvenated. As the book nears its close, a false happiness is being built upon a foundation of lies. Hardy's penchant for the grotesque is shown once again in the appearance of the effigy at the moment of Henchard's thoughts of suicide.

Hardy's belief in the power of music is shown in the passage where Henchard's despair is deepest: "If he could have summoned music to his aid, his existence might even now have been borne."

QUESTION

Do you believe in Henchard's optimistic remark at the end of the chapter?

CHAPTER 42

SYNOPSIS: FARFRAE AND ELIZABETH-JANE MEET AGAIN

About a year passes. Farfrae, not knowing of Jopp's malevolence, puts aside any plans to punish the perpetrators of the skimmity-ride. Henchard now owns a small seed shop purchased for him by the town council. Together he and Elizabeth-Jane begin to make a respectable living for themselves. However, even though Henchard has come to disregard the eventuality of Newson's return, he now fears that Donald Farfrae will wish to marry Elizabeth-Jane, thus robbing him of the only creature close to him. He has seen many newly-bought books in Elizabeth-Jane's modest room and wonders how she has been able to buy them.

Farfrae, in time, has come to believe that Lucetta's secret would have come out sooner or later, and if she had lived their chances for happiness would probably not have been so great.

Donald and Elizabeth-Jane begin to meet, accidentally at first. Donald continues to give her presents of books, and soon their old love grows anew. Henchard spies on them, burning with a kind of possessive jealousy. His suspicions are justified when he sees Donald kissing Elizabeth-Jane, and for a fleeting moment he considers telling Donald of his stepdaughter's illegitimate birth. But he cannot quite bring himself to do it and exclaims: "Why should I still be subject to these visitations of the devil . . . ?"

DISCUSSION

Farfrae is now depicted by Hardy as a rather prim and somewhat unforgiving man. Though he has shown forgiveness to Henchard and an understanding of humanity in the past, his rueful thoughts about Lucetta seem to give him almost a puritanical air. This tends to give more weight to Henchard's thought that Farfrae might drop Elizabeth-Jane if he knew of her birth, however.

Juno's bird   peacock
Argus eyes   mythological figure with one hundred eyes. When Argus was killed the eyes were placed on the tail of Juno's

sacred peacock.
solicitus timor   a worrisome fear (Latin)
locus standi   accepted or recognized standing (Latin)

QUESTION

Why does Farfrae, who has never been unkind or unfair, seem like a lesser man than Henchard, who has been inconsiderate, untruthful, and even dishonorable throughout the story?

CHAPTER 43

SYNOPSIS: HENCHARD LEAVES CASTERBRIDGE

Henchard realizes that the town is filled with gossip about Donald and Elizabeth-Jane. The "philosophic party" among the rustics are the only ones entirely pleased at the thought of their marriage. Henchard begins to worry about the life he will lead once the two are married. One day he goes to spy with a telescope on Donald and Elizabeth-Jane, but discovers Newson waiting instead of the two lovers. Henchard returns and Elizabeth-Jane tells him of a letter she has received requesting her to meet a stranger on the Budmouth Road or at Farfrae's house in the evening. Henchard realizes that the stranger is Newson come to claim his daughter. Michael immediately says to her "as if he did not care about her" that he is leaving Casterbridge. Despite her pleas, Henchard will not reconsider and at dusk he leaves town, once more as an itinerant hay-trusser. She accompanies him a short distance and sadly bids him farewell. As she is returning to Casterbridge, Donald meets her and brings her to his home where she is reunited with Newson. After Newson informs her that Henchard had lied about her death, Elizabeth-Jane's feelings toward Henchard grow cold and bitter. She and Donald actually turn against Michael so strongly that Newson takes his part. However, the past is put aside for the moment and preparations for the wedding are begun.

DISCUSSION

One wonders how Newson had discovered Farfrae and Elizabeth-Jane. Hardy leaves out this incident possibly to prevent the inclusion of another chance occurrence. Yet Hardy may have skipped over these details to bring the climactic moment to a faster resolution and to make a number of points. The focus remains of Henchard and his emotional suffering. Because Henchard has learned to sacrifice for love and is truly suffering in expiation for his sins, the sympathy shifts directly upon him, and the reader begins to experience a more intense pity for the one-time esteemed Mayor of Casterbridge.

éclat distinction or brilliance (French)
Mai Dun a large fortress of the ancient Britons
via road, path (Latin)
Cain in *Genesis:* for killing his brother Abel, Cain was branded (Mark of Cain) and cursed by God to wander among men, and to be shunned by them.
schiedam gin (named after the town in Holland where it had been made)

QUESTION

What does Newson's response to Henchard's lie about Elizabeth-Jane reveal about his character?

CHAPTER 44

SYNOPSIS: HENCHARD BRINGS A WEDDING GIFT

Dressed as he was when he first came to Casterbridge, Henchard makes his way for six days to Weydon-Priors. There he re-enacts in his mind the events of his original rash deed and the consequences of it. He is unable to shake off his constant thoughts of Elizabeth-Jane. Finally he obtains work as a hay-trusser at a place about fifty miles by direct road from Casterbridge. As the days pass he comes to think of the possibility that Newson might not have come to reclaim his daughter. He decides that he may have acted rashly and determines to go to her wedding after surmising from the talk of travelers that its date is St. Martin's Day. Two days before the wedding he leaves on foot for Casterbridge, determined not to arrive until evening of the wedding-day.

Henchard stops at the town of Shottsford to purchase new clothes for himself and a gift of a goldfinch in a cage for Elizabeth-Jane. Henchard arrives after the wedding and waits outside town for dark to fall. That evening Farfrae's house is filled with music and gaiety. Henchard inquires after Mr. and Mrs. Farfrae at the back entrance of the house and momentarily deposits the goldfinch beneath a bush. While waiting for Elizabeth-Jane, he sees her and Donald dancing gaily. Suddenly he is aware of a new partner dancing with Elizabeth-Jane. He recognizes Newson, and Henchard's hopes are dashed. However, before he has a chance to leave, Elizabeth-Jane comes out. Her first surprised remark: "Oh—it is—Mr. Henchard!" Henchard is stung by the formality of the way she has addressed him and pleads for her to keep a little love in her heart. But Elizabeth-Jane cannot forgive him and accuses him of deceit. Henchard does not even attempt to defend himself, but apologizes for having caused her discomfort at his appearance: "I have done wrong in coming to 'ee—I see my error. But it is only for once, so forgive it. I'll never trouble 'ee again, Elizabeth-Jane—no, not to my dying day! Good-night. Good-bye!" With this Henchard leaves Elizabeth-Jane forever.

DISCUSSION

This chapter is the last to depict Henchard's dogged attempts to find love and affection. It was, of course, self-delusion on his part to persuade himself that Newson had not returned to claim Elizabeth-Jane. Throughout the book Michael Henchard is wrong in all his choices and all his plans. Yet, in the last few chapters one thought refuses to leave him. He believes that despite his persistent attempts to show Elizabeth-Jane deep and abiding love, she will not forgive him when Newson reclaims her. In this one instance—irony of ironies—he is absolutely right.

quickset hawthorn hedges
of aught besides of anything
  else, also
pixy-ring a fairy-ring. A term
  given to the area or ring on the
  meadow where a different type
  of grass is growing

pari passu at the same speed
  (Latin)
Martin's Day November 11th
sequestration seclusion
Samson shorn from *Judges*. A
  strong man who has been robbed
  of his strength

QUESTION

Why does this chapter seem sadder than the many others
in which Henchard has suffered misfortune?

CHAPTER 45

SYNOPSIS: AN OBSCURE DESTINY

It is about a month after the night of the wedding reception. Elizabeth-Jane has grown somewhat accustomed to her
new position. Newson has gone to live at Budmouth in sight
of the sea. A maid tells Elizabeth-Jane that they now know who
had abandoned the birdcage near the back entrance. One week
after her marriage Elizabeth-Jane had found the birdcage and
the starved goldfinch. She had been terribly upset by the discovery. The servant informs her that it was the "farmer's man
who called on the evening of the wedding." Elizabeth-Jane
realizes that Henchard had brought her a gift and feels anguish
at her harshness to him. She and Donald set out to find him,
and even though they travel a great distance in search of the
man who had apparently "sunk into the earth," their efforts
are fruitless. However, a good many miles from Casterbridge
they discover Abel Whittle entering a cottage which is "of
humble dwellings surely the humblest." They learn from Abel
that Michael has died within the half-hour. Abel had followed
Michael the night of the wedding reception and had taken care
of him during his sickness, because Henchard had been kind
to his mother when she was alive. He shows Elizabeth-Jane
Henchard's crudely written but deeply moving will. Michael
Henchard's last requests are that no formal ceremonies accompany his burial and that Elizabeth-Jane not be informed of his
death. Though Elizabeth-Jane now feels deep sorrow at having

been unkind to Michael, she nevertheless respects his strong determination and abides by the rude testament. She devotes the rest of her life to her husband and to the needs of the less fortunate.

DISCUSSION

This chapter shows Michael Henchard as a tragic figure. The reader understands that all Michael's sins have been expiated, not by his death, but through his suffering. His suffering, of course, is the direct result of his rash behavior as a young man. Yet there is an ennobling quality about his last actions, since they are motivated by love of another human being. His love and kindness toward Elizabeth-Jane are mirrored in Abel Whittle's tender care and devotion.

The symbolism of the starved goldfinch is quite effective since Henchard, himself, becomes sick and is unable to take nourishment. Furthermore, an added subtextual symbol is evident in the fact that Henchard, too, is starved to death for want of Elizabeth-Jane's love.

antipodean absences absences on the other side of the world. Probably the phrase refers to Australian penal colonies.

assize town a town where civil and criminal cases are tried by jury

Minerva-eyes . . . face the sense is that Elizabeth-Jane has acquired wisdom, and that she imparts the spirit of wisdom in her movements.

Diana Multimammia many-breasted Diana. The sense is that the burial-mounds appeared to be the many breasts.

Capharnaum from *Matthew*; place of darkness

QUESTION

How would you analyze each term of Henchard's will?

CRITICAL ANALYSIS

STRUCTURE

The Mayor of Casterbridge is one of Thomas Hardy's most unified works. Never for a moment is Michael Henchard out of our minds. Even when whole chapters are devoted to Donald Farfrae, Lucetta Templeman, Elizabeth-Jane, or some of the minor characters, Michael Henchard's strength of character lingers on each page like bass notes of impending doom. And indeed, this is how it should be, for Hardy subtitled his novel *A Story of a Man of Character*.

Hardy does not attempt to qualify Henchard's "character" as good or bad. His structure rests on the effect of Henchard's character upon his own life and the lives of others. It is certainly this element more than others that makes the novel stand out amidst the many Victorian novels whose important characters are less powerfully conceived than Henchard or all too easily disappear early and return from obscurity two hundred pages later. Susan's ruined life is a direct result of Henchard's rashness; by extension, Elizabeth-Jane owes her very existence to Henchard's folly; Donald Farfrae receives his start from Henchard, and indeed Henchard's wild speculations and superstitious nature only help to advance Farfrae; and Lucetta's death is a direct outcome of her past relationship with Henchard. Hardy did not require us to like Michael Henchard; however, he has so structured the novel that we cannot forget him. Henchard *is* the novel.

How is it, then, that the other characters in the novel keep our attention? In the case of Donald and Elizabeth-Jane, the reader knows they will marry before the end of the novel. Concerning Lucetta, the reader is thoroughly aware that she will not marry Henchard. It is only the pitfalls and vicissitudes of their lives that provide interest and suspense. Thus our interest in these characters is aroused in direct proportion to the catalytic effect that Henchard's character and behavior have in motivating their actions.

Throughout the novel is felt the influence of *King Lear,* Shakespeare's massive tragedy. One recalls that Lear rashly disowns his true and loving daughter, falls from the heights of regality into suffering and madness, and is briefly reconciled with her before his death. The realization of this structural parallel strengthens our knowledge that the unity of the work is predicated on Henchard's character. After all, his rashness precipitates the events which, once started, move unrelentingly on.

The first two chapters of the novel and the very last serve as a frame for the core of the novel's story. The opening chapters display the unhappy events that initiate the tale, and the last chapter rounds them off, thus bringing the plot full circle. That is, Henchard enters the novel impoverished and miserable, but young, vigorous, and still master of his own fate. In the last chapter he departs from the novel—and from this world—more impoverished, more wretched, barely in his middle-age, master of nothing. If the novel had begun with Henchard already established as mayor, the sale of his wife, if pulled out of the closet of obscurity as an old family skeleton, would make the story preposterous.

It was apparently not completely possible for Hardy to escape some of the seemingly melodramatic, and at times forced, incidents which abound in the fiction of his era. Henchard speculates wildly in order to destroy Farfrae, and the weather changes; the "furmity woman" shows up and causes Michael's complete downfall; Newson returns from the dead and destroys the ex-mayor's only chance for happiness.

Nevertheless, though these untoward events may seem heavily weighted on the side of the novelist's plot development, none of them is really incredible. Even Henchard cannot control the weather. What person would not remember the face of the man who sold his wife to the highest bidder (and since the "furmity woman" is a vagabond type, she could easily turn up in Casterbridge as well as anywhere else)? Is it not natural for Newson to attempt to reclaim his own child in order to bestow his fortune upon her as his heir? These events are justified, although the modern reader may be disturbed by the machinations behind them.

In this vein there are also at least four overheard conversations: Lucetta overhears Henchard reading her letters, and she naturally fears that Donald will surmise her past history; Henchard, earlier, hides behind a stack of wheat and listens to Donald and Lucetta's passionate conversation; Donald and Lucetta listen intently to the two parting lovers in the market, thus uniting their spirits in a romantic bond; and finally, Henchard, once again from hiding, overhears Donald addressing Elizabeth-Jane in tender words and knows the meeting has ended with a kiss. If the reader has assumed that these overheard conversations are melodramatic tricks, let him also note that such tricks are more melodramatic if the listener *accidentally* overhears. However, in these cases, each of the listeners *purposely* eavesdrops.

The comparative abundance of coincidences, returns from the past, secret letters, and the like, should not lead the reader to think that Hardy has mismanaged his realism. There are many realistic elements in the novel (modern critics tend to think that Hardy's realism of dialogue, precise descriptions of buildings and countryside, etc., are false criteria of his excellence), but the importance of *The Mayor of Casterbridge* is now generally assumed to lie outside its fidelity to the canons of painstaking realism, either of setting or incident. One critic sees in the sequence of events the working out of a scheme of retribution by an outraged moral order in the universe. Another sees in Henchard an astonishingly perceptive treatment of the character unconsciously bent on his own destruction, in this anticipating the findings of modern psychology. In either event, mere plausibility of structure appears of negligible importance.

POINT OF VIEW AND STYLE

Hardy's narrative style is that of the *omniscient* or *ubiquitous* narrator. This gives him a point of view that allows him to comment upon the vagaries of nature, to place himself in the mind of a character in order to give us reasons and motives, and to philosophize or describe the background to clarify whatever point he wishes to make. In short, Hardy knows all and is everywhere in *The Mayor of Casterbridge,* although we learn only what he wants us to know. When we have finished the novel, our thoughts about it are to some extent what Hardy wants us to think.

Hardy's actual writing style is usually clear and is often extremely well wrought. If an occasional awkward sentence or overly long descriptive passage comes to light, perhaps we should reflect upon the conventions of the era in which he wrote. The comparative infrequency of his lapses from clarity and economy may serve as a lesson for the student in "blue-penciling" or revision.

The opening pages of the novel display Hardy's ability to write admirable prose which delineates the personae, the background, and the circumstances from an omniscient narrator's point of view.

In the first two or three pages of the book we are treated to some excellent description, especially perhaps that of Susan's face. We also learn that the couple is unhappily married, the man is discontented, they are poor and somewhat shabby, and that Susan's philosophy toward life is rather pessimistic. Furthermore, the dry dust, the barren countryside, and the "blackened-green stage of colour" of the vegetation lend an oppressive air to the scene as a prelude to the dark events to come. Hardy reveals his somber mastery of setting, mood, and character throughout the novel, and the reader rarely has to search for clarity.

Hardy's ability with dialogue is evident on two levels. The dialogue reflects his characters' social position while it adds to our knowledge of their personalities. A passage from Chapter 9 will illustrate this.

"Now I am not the man to let a cause be lost for want of a word. And before ye are gone for ever I'll speak. Once more, will ye stay? There it is, flat and plain. You can see that it isn't all selfishness that makes me press 'ee; for my business is not quite so scientific as to require an intellect entirely out of the common. Others would do for the place without doubt. Some selfishness perhaps there is, but there is more; it isn't for me to repeat what. Come bide with me—and name your own terms. I'll agree to 'em willingly and 'ithout a word gainsaying; for, hang it, Farfrae, I like thee well!"

This example shows Henchard's very blunt character. Not a word is wasted, and he comes directly to the point. He uses countrified expressions but does not speak like the lower-class townspeople. Furthermore, the impetuous nature of his character is shown in both speeches by his vehement attempt to hire Farfrae because he likes him and to press upon Donald his immediate friendship, without the normal preliminaries, by insisting that he come to breakfast.

Farfrae's kind and fair disposition is amply brought out by a number of his speeches, although he is almost never given a very long speech. Farfrae's reasonableness and sweetness become somewhat cloying in the light of the struggles and transformation which Henchard is undergoing. Nevertheless, his unwillingness to commit an act of blatant vengeance or meanness, and his Scottish economy of speech are distinctly brought forth in these passages from Chapter 34.

"About that little seedsman's shop," he said; "the shop overlooking the churchyard, which is to let. It is not for myself I want it, but for our unlucky fellow-townsman Henchard. It would be a new beginning for him, if a small one; and I have told the Council that I would head a private subscription among them to set him up in it—that I would be fifty pounds, if they would make up the other fifty among them."

"But I cannet discharge a man who was once a good friend to me? How can I forget that when I came here 'twas he enabled me to make a footing for mysel'? No, no. As long as I've a day's wark to offer he shall do it if he chooses. 'Tis not I who will deny him such a little as that. But I'll drop the idea of establishing him in a shop till I can think more about it."

The letters of Lucetta Templeman are quite as revealing as most of her speeches. The reader wonders why she would be so reckless as to write such candid letters to Henchard. Her candor bespeaks a certain naïveté or trust on her part, but it also shows an element of abandon which Hardy carefully traces to her *French* background. The letters and her bantering with Farfrae show a certain sophisticated ability to play with words in a teasing manner. To Hardy—though not to us today—this is enough to characterize Lucetta with what was to the English mind French sensuality or even licentiousness. The following passages from Chapter 23 catch her character brilliantly.

"I mean all you Scotchmen," she added in hasty correction. "So free from Southern extremes. We common people are all one way or the other—warm or cold, passionate or frigid. You have both temperatures going on in you at the same time."

"It is very hard," she said with strong feelings. "Lovers ought not
to be parted like that! Oh, if I had my wish, I'd let people live and
love at their pleasure!"

"It is kind-hearted of you, indeed," said Lucetta. "For my part, I
have resolved that all my servants shall have lovers if they want them!
Do make the same resolve!"

Through her speech, Hardy shows the gradual change that
takes place in Elizabeth-Jane through the years. At first she has
a somewhat natural bent toward good times and playfulness,
although she never appears giddy. As her sorrows increase, she
turns more and more to study and reflection. At the end of the
novel the reader finds Elizabeth-Jane characterized somewhat as
a melancholy, kind, matronly woman whose speech seems
highly studied and affected, even when her words are deeply
emotional:

She flushed up, and gently drew her hand away. "I could have
loved you always—I would have, gladly," said she. "But how can I
when I know you have deceived me so—so bitterly deceived me! You
persuaded me that my father was not my father—allowed me to live
on in ignorance of the truth for years; and then when he, my warm-
hearted real father, came to find me, cruelly sent him away with a
wicked invention of my death, which nearly broke his heart. O how
can I love as I once did a man who has served us like this!"

As far as the lower-class types are concerned, Hardy has
characterized them as mischievous knaves who often speak in
vulgar terms. Yet, they have a vigorous life of their own, and
Hardy has revealed with enormous skill the picturesque qualities
that can only be found in authentic folk dialect.

Another aspect of Hardy's over-all style is his fondness for
Gothic atmosphere—that is, secret meetings or plots or incidents occurring in gloomy or melancholy surroundings. The
opening chapter of the book has this quality to it, as does
Henchard's meeting with Susan at the Ring, and his discovery
of the "skimmity-ride" figure in the water. With little difficulty
the student can probably recall at least two more incidents or
surroundings that indicate a *Gothic* treatment.

In its wealth of realistic detail, Hardy's descriptive style
created his Wessex world with such conviction and thoroughness
that he became the model for dozens of other regional novelists.
His realism is not now appreciated as much as his more tragic,

universal qualities, but it contributes substantially in *The Mayor of Casterbridge* to the total tragic effect. Henchard is considered by at least one critic to be the only genuinely successful attempt at a tragic hero in the modern novel. But Henchard is so embedded in the real world of grain dealing, furmity, seed lips, stout breakfasts, and hay bales as to have for the modern reader an affinity with his own experience that other romantic heroes, enveloped in myth and legend, do not. As tragic hero he is of a stature comparable with theirs, but he comes to us, as it were, in the homely corduroy of a hay-trusser rather than in cape or toga. In part because of Hardy's Wessex realism, Henchard is a tragic hero we can touch.

THEME

The theme of *The Mayor of Casterbridge* appears to be the arbitrary and almost always malign workings of the universe and blind chance upon the destinies of men. Such evil, unrelenting machinations bring pain and suffering upon the characters in the novel, and there is no escape except in a day-to-day acceptance of life.

Much has been written concerning Hardy's famous pessimism. However, in *The Mayor of Casterbridge,* despite the workings of blind fate, the occurrences of chance, and the vagaries of a hostile natural environment, Michael Henchard is still responsible for his own fate. If he had not sold his wife in a fit of drunken self-pity, the painful events would not have ensued. If he had not overspeculated in order to ruin Farfrae, it would not have mattered if it rained, or snowed, or hailed. Certainly in his many years as corn-factor and leading business-man he had come through other natural disasters. It is only in this one case that he lets his keen sense of rivalry and lust for revenge cause him to speculate recklessly.

Nor is Hardy indifferent to man's senseless cruelty to his brother. He structures the events so that even Elizabeth-Jane has become too prim and unrelenting in her firm stand on Lucetta and Henchard. He is unsparing in his portrayal of the lower-class townspeople for their cruel and vicious "skimmity-ride." And, in Henchard's case, since he is the focal point of the novel, Hardy is saying that wickedness and evil will return to the perpetrator in full cycle, in like measure. He is indeed saying that the evil which man does will not only live after him, but it—evil, not fate—will dog man's steps until poetic justice has been satisfied.

One last word. Let the reader observe Henchard's behavior after Elizabeth-Jane has come to dwell with him, and the motivations for that behavior. Though Henchard's actions are somewhat tempered with the base emotion of jealousy—which is only human—all that he does is motivated by love of Elizabeth-Jane. He lies to Newson because he doesn't want to lose Elizabeth-Jane; he leaves Casterbridge because he cannot bear Elizabeth-Jane's scorn; he returns to show his love and to be forgiven; he departs forever so as not to cause his foster-daughter pain and embarrassment; and finally, he writes a will whose requirements will blot out his existence from the eyes of men, especially from Elizabeth-Jane whom he does not wish to hurt. There is nobility in Henchard because he willingly takes upon himself suffering as an expiation for the sins of his life. He carries his suffering and his love for Elizabeth-Jane in silence. And when man can rise to stature and nobility as Henchard does at the end of *The Mayor of Casterbridge,* then the dominant chord Hardy has struck swells to a bold theme of hope for mankind.

CHARACTER SKETCHES

Michael Henchard

Michael Henchard is a strong man with great energy. He has fine points in his character, but they are contrasted sharply with other less admirable qualities. Thus, he will try to make up for what he has done to Susan, but he will still remain rash and impetuous in his dealings with people. He is honest and upright, so much so that he insists on binding one of his arms when fighting Farfrae, and he refuses to hide one cent of his property from the administrators of his bankrupt business. Even the administrators praise his honesty. He is generous and kind to Abel Whittle's mother. Donald Farfrae owes much to Henchard's giving him a start. These are but a few instances of Henchard's honesty and generosity.

But the darker side of Henchard's character is even more evident. He has no compunction in punishing Abel Whittle too severely for lateness, and the quality of his kindness and friendship to Farfrae becomes overbearing and possessive. His pride is noteworthy, but often it grows into hideous egoism. Thus, his pride refuses to let him reveal his past to Elizabeth-Jane, and at the end of the novel he cannot bring himself to tell her the true account of his lie to Newson. Again, it is his pride which prompts the rivalry and jealousy he feels toward Donald Farfrae. But, despite obvious flaws in his character, Henchard has the ability to love deeply. He achieves the strength to take silently upon himself the suffering caused by his own sins, and it is this will to endure the wrath of the heavens that gives him great stature.

Susan

Hardy purposely drew Susan as a vague character. Before the end of the third chapter it becomes clear that she has suffered an outrage not to be endured. If her character were outlined more definitely, Hardy would be running the risk of displacing the focus from Henchard to Susan and give her a more assertive part in the plot. Thus it is unnecessary to speculate on what her life would have been like if Henchard had not auctioned her off. It is clear, however, that her simple nature lends her an innocence and trust that almost surpass the bounds of credibility. She believes pessimistically that the events of her life have been structured by an unkind fate, and she does not look to mankind for assistance.

Elizabeth-Jane

Elizabeth-Jane, tempered in poverty and the loss of her father, Newson, and her mother, resigns herself to study and self-betterment. Her beauty begins to flower with the more wholesome diet and relatively relaxed atmosphere of living in a wealthy home. She senses something improper in Susan and Henchard's past relationship, and almost unconsciously she strives to emulate a conservative, formal, correct social relationship with others. However, despite the melancholy aura which surrounds her, Elizabeth-Jane is able to love deeply and sincerely. In fact, she has observed so much of life around her with such an understanding eye that she cannot remain bitter in any way. Even when she renounces Henchard for lying to her about Newson—an understandable action considering her deep love for Newson—she cannot long remain bitter and sets out to find him. Her tribute to Henchard's memory is in honoring his last wishes since she knows that he was a man of indomitable will. She dedicates the rest of her life to kindness, humanity, and learning, and her soul becomes more beautiful as she advances through life.

Donald Farfrae

Donald Farfrae is a young Scotsman, leaner and frailer than Henchard. However, what he lacks in physical strength, he more than makes up for in charm, wit, and good humor. Donald has a mind for mechanical things and business. But, whereas Henchard has no penchant for creative endeavors, Donald has cultivated a pleasant singing voice and knows how to give an entertainment that will appeal to others. The most pronounced contrast between Henchard's and Donald's characters is that Donald cannot truly harbor a grudge or wish to be vengeful. He is prudent in his philosophy and social outlook, and one feels that he and Elizabeth-Jane are manifestly suited to each other.

Lucetta Templeman (Le Sueur)

In Victorian times, Lucetta would have been considered a reckless libertine. Today we would call her a rather flighty, flirtatious, indiscreet young lady. There is not much depth to Lucetta's character once we place her beside Elizabeth-Jane. She writes compromising letters to Henchard and takes her married life in her hands when she meets him secretly at the Ring. But she does not think of these things until it is too late. She is preoccupied with clothing, comfort, fashions, and sophisticated light banter. She is quick to deny Donald's former connection with Henchard during the disturbance of the royal visitor, and her rather snobbish attitude turns Jopp into a bitter enemy who plots her downfall. In short, the lack of depth in her personality is shown in Donald's own thoughts when he realizes, after her death, that he would not have been happy with her.

Newson

Newson, if we are to accept the statements of Susan and Elizabeth-Jane, is a kind, jovial man. We are given a demonstration of his kindness—or forgiving nature—when he refuses to chastise Henchard for lying to him. His trusting nature is shown again when he takes Henchard's word at face value and departs without even visiting the cemetery. Yet he is thoughtful of others. The story of his loss at sea is a kindly deception by which he will give Susan the freedom to return to Henchard.

Jopp

Jopp is a dark character who possesses no wit, business sense, or honor. What is clearest about his character is his ability to harbor a grudge and to take joy in seeing an enemy suffer. His function in the novel is at once to serve as a villain and a catalyst for villainous behavior.

Abel Whittle

At first singled out for his extreme simplicity, Abel Whittle becomes more the faithful follower than the scatterbrain as the story develops. From the clownish bumpkin of the trousers episode he becomes in his fidelity to the dying Henchard a figure comparable to Lear's Fool. His care for Henchard is an ironic instance of the completeness of Henchard's fall, for Abel, the lowliest character in the book, is Henchard's last tie to humanity.

Minor Characters

There are a number of rustics who not only provide atmosphere but act something like a chorus in Greek drama. Through Mrs. Cuxsom, Nance Mockridge, Christopher Coney, and Solomon Longways, the reader gets a feeling of the community, not only as it is but how it feels. These characters are partly individualized, Nance being low and spiteful, and Solomon, like his Biblical namesake, aspiring toward a judicious outlook on events.

NOTES